PENGUIN LIFE

## THE ULTIMATE STAY-AT-HOME DAD

Shannon Carpenter has been a stay-at-home dad since 2008. He is also a humor writer trained through the famous Second City. Whether writing social satire or parenting essays, he is always able to find your funny bone and leave you with a lasting impression. He has done public readings on local NPR affiliate KCUR and teaching through the National At-Home Dad Network, and the Dad 2.0 national conference, which named him one of the funniest dads of 2019. He has also given interviews about his experiences to *Forbes, The Wall Street Journal,* and *The New York Times,* as well as his local NBC and FOX stations. *Redbook* magazine named him one of America's "Adventure Dads." Finally, *BuzzFeed* recognized him as one of the funniest women of the week in 2020, which was weird because he is not a woman. However, he is very funny.

# THE ULTIMATE STAY-AT-HOME DAD

## Your Essential Manual for Being an Awesome Full-Time Father

**SHANNON CARPENTER**

life

PENGUIN BOOKS

An imprint of Penguin Random House LLC

penguinrandomhouse.com

A Penguin Life Book

LIBRARY OF CONGRESS CATALOGING-IN-PUBLICATION DATA

Names: Carpenter, Shannon (Humorist), author.
Title: The ultimate stay-at-home dad: your essential manual for being an
   awesome full-time father / Shannon Carpenter.
Identifiers: LCCN 2020057464 (print) | LCCN 2020057465 (ebook) |
   ISBN 9780143135647 (trade paperback) | ISBN 9780525507321 (ebook)
Subjects: LCSH: Stay-at-home fathers. | Fatherhood—Humor. |
   Parenting—Humor.
Classification: LCC HQ756.6 .C37 2021 (print) | LCC HQ756.6 (ebook) |
   DDC 306.874/2—dc23
LC record available at https://lccn.loc.gov/2020057464
LC ebook record available at https://lccn.loc.gov/2020057465

Printed in the United States of America
1st Printing

Set in Sabon MT Std
Designed by Cassandra Garruzzo

*For Vivi, Wyatt, Ollie, Luke, Rory, Cait, Ella, Sam, Audra, Asher, Eli, Abby, Adam, Luke, Lydia, and Anna.*

*Let's go on another adventure.*

# CONTENTS

# THE
# ULTIMATE
# STAY-AT-HOME
# DAD

CHAPTER 1

# EMBRACING FATHERHOOD

Congratulations on your promotion to an at-home dad!
Your new job pays nothing, starts at midnight, and
there are no sick days. You'll love it.

What comes to mind when you hear the term *stay-at-home dad*? Let me help you out. It's either a lazy dude or Mr. Mom, and neither are pleasant.

The first one is a guy who hasn't bathed in a year and wears a brown sweater that has holes around the neckline. There are kids somewhere in a dirty and destroyed house. Dinner is never on the table at six, the wife works three jobs to support his ass, and occasionally he will tear himself away from *World of Warcraft* to ask for beer money.

If that's not the one, then your mind goes to the 1983 movie *Mr. Mom*, starring Michael Keaton. I have a soft spot for that movie because my own wife is in advertising, and it's funny as hell. I get it. But the term *Mr. Mom* oozes with this vision of a dad without a manly bone in his body. It implies that his masculinity has been stripped and his balls have been replaced by fallopian tubes. He's no longer a guy because he has decided to take on the role of raising children. In short, the term supposes that he can't be Dad because he is now Mom.

I've been an at-home dad for twelve years, and I can safely tell you all of that is complete and total bullshit.

That's not who we are. That's not even close.

## WORDS OF WISDOM

The cliché in the world is that an at-home dad is lazy and worthless. At least, that is the mental picture that dads wrestle with because of the looks and reactions we get when we respond to "What do you do for a living?" But as dads, we do not have to accept this preconceived notion because it is not true. We are worth every penny to our family. I used to answer "What do you do for a living?" with hesitation, but I'm now confident in my role and in our decision as a family for me to be an at-home dad.

*Brock Lusch, father of two*

At-home dads are salesmen, IT specialists, and marketing managers. We are doctors and lawyers, mechanics and electricians. Some have college degrees, and some don't. We are blue collar and white collar, big house and small house, bearded with tattoos and clean shaven. Some ride motorcycles; others ride imaginary unicorns, to their daughters' delight. Some drink whiskey and beer, and some abstain with a vitaminwater.

We can chop wood with huge axes and run a sewing machine to make special pillows for our newborn sons. Some of us are loud and outgoing, and others are shy and withdrawn. We are aggressive and passive, sure of ourselves and not.

We are every guy you've ever met.

As you read this book, you'll start seeing how diverse stay-at-home dads really are. We come from every walk of life, every religion, every race, every orientation. There are fathers of twins and triplets, fathers of trans children, fathers of special needs kids. Some are newer guys with a year's worth of experience, and some have been doing this for decades. This is now your community and we are here to help, to give you a sense of the importance of what you do, and to teach you everything we know about being an at-home dad. There are dads with wives, dads with husbands, and dads with partners. In this book, you will see yourself.

In these pages, I'll focus on the one unifying factor that brings us all together. We are Dad. Are we Mr. Mom? Only if we can start calling Mom Mrs. Dad. See how well that shit plays out. Stay-at-home dads are a community bigger than you could possibly know, but closer than you ever thought.

There are over two million of us in the US alone, and that is using a very strict definition. Those dads who have part-time jobs aren't "officially" at-home dads, which the rest of us say is bullshit. Driving for a rideshare company on the weekend does not exclude you from the club.

We are the dads who don't see Mom as a problem, the kid as an obstacle, and fatherhood as an unfortunate side effect of sex. Being Dad isn't something that someone else can do. It's what *we* do. We are the primary caregivers of our children. Period.

Those are the men you are joining. Millions. Say it with me: millions. The hero from the Disney movie *The Incredibles 2*, Mr. Incredible? At-home dad. The movie star Cary Grant did a stint in the parenting trenches. Rick Moranis? At-home dad. That's right, Dark Helmet himself is an at-home dad. May his greatness live forever.

Now we can begin to understand how to answer the question "What do you do for a living?"

## "WHAT DO YOU DO FOR A LIVING?" WHAT TO SAY WHEN YOUR JOB DESCRIPTION IS JUST "EVERYTHING."

I am an excellent storyteller.

"I'm a stunt car driver out in LA," I said to the very nice lady at my wife's high school reunion. "Well, I guess you can call it Hollywood, but it sounds so pretentious. Know what I mean?"

"Are you really?" she asked, obviously impressed. She twirled the champagne in her glass.

"Oh, yeah," I said. "That's why I shave my head bald. Hair is a fire hazard, ya know. That fire-retardant hair cream doesn't work as well as you would think."

None of it is true, of course. That line about shaving my head might have been too much. It was good, though.

"So, what movies have I seen you in?" she asked.

"Well, let's see . . . ," I began. Then I was called on my bullshit.

"Good God, he's not a stunt car driver." Everyone, meet my wife, Erin. She routinely calls me on my crap but also enjoys my stories. She's very conflicted.

"Oh," my wife's old school chum said as she stopped swirling her champagne. "So, what *do* you do for a living then?"

Fuck. There it was, the question that many of us at-home dads dread at the beginning. At the time, I wasn't comfortable answering it, thus the awesome story about being a stunt car driver. Although there is truth to be gleaned from that story. Have you ever driven down a dirt road while having cereal thrown at your head by a toddler with a god complex? I've done that while also answering *Jeopardy!*-like questions about why the sky is blue and whether cows really fart.

So, in a very technical sense, I *am* a stunt car driver. I am also a cook, cleaner, behavioral specialist, chief diaper changer, toddler wrangler, baby vomit hazmat team, human play gym, and belly-flop champion, thank you very much.

"I stay home with the kids," I said to the champagne-sipping lady. In my head, eyes around the ballroom started to glare. I wasn't terribly worried—all the people my wife went to high school with are very small. I could probably take a good ten to twenty of them at once.

False bravado is pretty much how I get through any uncomfortable situation, by the way.

"You're unemployed?" she asked.

Double fuck.

This is the problem in the beginning when you tell people you quit your job to raise your family. They quickly assume that I'm unemployed. People tend to go immediately to the cliché, the myth in popular culture of the stay-at-home dad. It all stems from our very acronym. SAHD = sad. There was a touch of sympathy in her voice that seemed to say, "You poor dear. Are you looking for work? It can be tough out there." She sipped champagne once again, her social status now confirmed and the unemployed liar exposed.

"No, I'm not unemployed," I said. "My job is to take care of two kids. That's what I do."

"And he does a wonderful job," my wife said. She reacted differently to the question than I did. Erin was proud. "With two kids under three, we wanted to have someone home with them. He's amazing." She grabbed my arm and gave it a squeeze. "He's way better at it than I am." Boom. That's her mic drop, and her friend looked confused for a minute. Maybe the champagne had gone bad.

She's also right. I am way better at being at home with the kids. I have three kids at home with me now, Vivi, Wyatt, and Oliver. They rock because I rock. Probably. I'm sure my wife had something to do with it. But admitting what I did for a living, to truly own it, didn't come naturally to me. My wife could answer the question way better than I could.

As I look back now, it's really hard to see myself as I once was. In my very crowded head, this first story stops with me ripping off my shirt and flexing. In that version of the story, my biceps are mountains and I have a full head of hair. I ride a valiant steed as I confront my wife's friends. I am Don Quixote fighting imaginary monsters. When I'm honest with myself, when I let the illusion fail, I arrive at the truth.

I was embarrassed.

At that point in time, I knew no other dads who stayed home with the kids. They all worked. Although I felt confident at home, out in the world I couldn't answer that question without a joke, and I had to deflect the truth. I felt exposed. I was afraid to discover that those imaginary monsters were only windmills after all and that I was a fool.

Twelve years later, I look back and realize that I was a fool, just not for the reason I thought then. It took me a while to learn what I needed to learn. So what do I know now that I didn't realize so many years earlier?

## Because Dad Says So . . .

*I have changed many diapers and let's just say I've seen things that will haunt me for the rest of my days. With parenting, you are going to get a lot wrong. Not a single parent out there really knows what they are doing. I will leave you with a bit of wisdom found where all wisdom is found, in a pop song: "Birds don't just fly. They fall down and get up." —Shakira*

**Bryan Alkire, father of two**

You have to own that shit. You're not asking for permission. You need to jump into the at-home dad role without remorse or apology. Your identity is not tied to a paycheck. It is rooted in the firm belief that what you do is best for your family. That is what I have learned. You are a Viking badass sailing to unknown shores in a minivan, and you do it with all of us cheering you on and waiting to hear your victory stories.

## FROM THE DADS GROUP

Oh yeah, we're all here ready to sing your praises and help you out. Everyone, meet Mick, Larry, Jake, and Mike. There's usually an initiation with cool hand-shakes, and then Mick drones on for about forty-five minutes with a prepared speech, but we can skip all that this time around. Welcome to your first dads group. This is how the guys answered the question "What do you do for a living?" when I asked them.

**MICK:** I'm an at-home dad. That's what I do. People get too wrapped up in this question. I could sit here and list out every task I do, but what's the point? What other people think of me doesn't matter.

**LARRY:** I do everything that needs to be done. [Larry is a man of few words. It's fantastic that he's in this book.]

**JAKE:** I mostly remind Shannon to keep his zipper up. It's like he forgot about it when he became an at-home dad. Oh, and take care of the kids. I do that a lot as well.

**MIKE:** Come down here after Shannon's funny little stories, and I'll tell you where he messed up, and how I would have done it better. When asked what you do, answer the question honestly and get straight to the point—don't beat around the bush: I'm an at-home dad.

All of us started out in the same place you are right now. We've all had to redefine ourselves. It wasn't always easy. And sometimes, it won't be for you.

Now do you know how to answer the question "What do you do for a living?" Do you know how to say what you do with confidence? Can you redefine yourself in your own head so that you can answer the question? It may not happen overnight, but you'll get there. You'll see the answer as surely as I did.

What do I do for a living?

I'm a motherfucking dad.

# TAKE CARE OF YOURSELF FIRST

All right, you badass, let's get to it. It's time to ignore everyone else and focus on you. I know it doesn't make sense. But as you are probably now finding out, it's a huge problem for the new at-home parent.

Being an at-home-parent means that you're pulled in every direction at the same time. Everyone wants something different, something now, and a lot of those somethings are not in your power to give. Some days it even feels like inanimate house chores are screaming at you. Maybe the house in *Amityville Horror* wasn't so bad; at least it shut its own windows and monitored the thermostat.

Through all of that, with every demand from every direction that is hitting you in the face, you've forgotten to take care of yourself.

None of this works without you. You need to come first.

## Because Dad Says So . . .

*To be the best parent you can be, you must take care of yourself first. Work on getting healthy physically, mentally, and emotionally, and you will become a better parent. YOU are part of the job as well, and many at-home dads forget that.*

**Al Watts, father of four**

All of us dads struggle with this. Hell, this is a universal parent problem. That's why the sweatpants business is still booming. It's the trap that we all fall into at one time or another. Being an at-home dad is a 24-7 job. There is no sick leave or company-approved vacation days, and you're going to get hit in the balls. Do this long enough and you'll start to fantasize about the hour-long traffic jam that you once took for granted. An hour by yourself with just your radio, and you don't even give a shit about how the wheels on the bus go round and round.

Let's focus on the tips for taking care of you first.

## BASIC HYGIENE

Look, this needs to be said even though you're thinking, *No shit, I need to take a shower.* Try that same thought after a week straight with no support and when the cartoon mascots are starting to talk to you.

> ### DAD HACK
> Look at joining a local community center or gym. Many have very cheap childcare for an hour. You can take your sweet time with a shower after your workout. It's nice to have time to yourself.

I've seen too many dads not spending enough time on their hygiene. It starts to affect your mental health. Trust me, I've been there. I know that even taking a shower when you have little ones can be a nightmare. I'm going to tell you my secret, and then we will be bros and we can awkwardly hug.

Get rid of the shower curtain.

Yup, that's what I did in the beginning. My first thirty days of being an at-home dad began with Erin leaving for a month. On day one, she boarded a plane, and I was home with a newborn and a nineteen-month-old. I had grand plans! There was going to be math, and classical music, and I was going to get Mr. Universe buff.

That fantasy lasted four days. That's how long it took to break me in the beginning. Four lousy days. I was up all night feeding Wyatt, my newborn, reheated breast milk. If he even heard the shower come on, he flipped out. He didn't care what time it was or how long he had been asleep. I would turn the nozzle and he would begin to scream.

I couldn't step into the shower during the day without either one of them absolutely losing their shit. So, I stumbled on my fix. I ditched the shower curtain so my six-week-old son, Wyatt, could still see me. My almost-two-year-old daughter played in the splash zone with the thousand Barbies that I gave her. That's how I did it. That's how I got my daily shower until I joined a gym that offered hour-long day care for a buck a kid.

Other dads have different solutions from what I did. Some wake up at five and get their shower in. Others wait until everyone is asleep, but I found that I needed the sleep as much as the kids did, especially when my wife was away on a business trip. Then there is the advice to "do it during nap time." This is solid advice, but parents are told to do everything at nap time. "Mow the lawn, then take a shower, clean the house, pay the bills, have the car washed, do your grocery shopping, and work on your Middle East peace plan during nap time." Seriously, how long is other parents' nap time? If you're solo, I stand by my no-shower-curtain rule when they are young.

Whatever you choose, make yourself a priority.

## THE WORKOUT

Now that you are showered, it's time to get to your actual physical health. That means exercise, which I will freely admit that I am horrible about. Luckily, I know guys who are great.

Working out doesn't have to be complicated, and if you pay attention in your neighborhood, you'll see the moms power walking with their strollers. A mile walk a day gets you out of the house and into the sunshine. And remember that you are Dad, which gives you certain superpowers.

I hiked a lot with my kids. I'm lucky enough to be in a part of the country that has extensive trails.

### DAD HACK

Look into hiking apps. There are plenty of great ones out there that will tell you everything you need to know about the trail, from elevation to the type of ground cover. And I would also recommend Star Walk, which shows the constellations on evening hikes. Amaze your toddler with pretty pictures while secretly teaching them.

Is that trail appropriate for a stroller? I dream of the stroller that comes with big truck mudding tires. If you are taking this route, ditch the stroller altogether and get a child-carrier backpack. If you have two children like I did then, throw the older kiddo on your shoulders, the younger one in the carrier, and hit the trail. However, make sure you try the backpack on IN THE STORE. My first one had a bar that dug into my lower back, which got worse when fifteen pounds of baby was added to the mix.

I know that fitting in any kind of workout or physical activity can be difficult. Believe me, I've lived it. Hell, I still live it. It's important because this is a marathon, not a sprint. You need to be able to do the same things that you are doing now in ten years. When everything seems to be falling apart, it's easier to just grab the doughnut and crash on the couch. Make time for your physical health, even if it's just a quick routine in the morning.

## Because Dad Says So . . .

*The important thing is to move regularly and remain active.*

*Perform these in a circuit of five rounds, resting sixty seconds between rounds:*

*20 push-ups*
*10 single-leg squat touchdowns (each leg)*
*20 mountain climbers*
*10 split squats (each leg)*
*30 seconds of high-knee run*

*To begin to get rid of the beer gut, start moving every day so that it becomes a habit. It can be as simple as taking a walk after you eat lunch or doing sit-ups, pushups, and squats when you wake up in the morning.*

**Michael Ashford, father of two**

## TIME WITHOUT FAMILY

One of the hardest parts of self-care, while you are at home with the kids, is getting any time for yourself. Some days it feels damn near impossible.

Get some low-cost hobbies and spend time with them. I do woodworking (we'll talk about incorporating your kids into this later). Others that I've seen are beer brewing (of course), gardening, lawn care (because we dads love telling people to get off our lawn), photography, and writing (a bit obvious for me). Whatever interest you have, set time aside for it every week and get your significant other on board. This is how you stave off burnout.

You must learn to separate the "you" from the "parent." This isn't even my own advice. This is what my therapist told me. Hell yes, I've gone to counseling just to check up on my own mental health. Shit gets complicated. There are ups and downs, and when you combine that with your own inadequacies and a winter-long snowstorm, things can look bleak. So, there you go—I've been to therapy several times over the last twelve years, and I'm a badass with a very healthy ego. My point is that you can be manly as fuck and still ask for mental health help. It's what made me a badass. The ego part is all me, though.

You have several "hats," as my therapist said. You need to wear all of them throughout the day. Sometimes that's the "dad" hat, in which I'm 100 percent focused on my kids. Other times, I have to put on the "Shannon" hat and it's all about me.

My wife and I have a rule in place that has worked very well over the years. Every day I get thirty minutes of "me" time, when I just walk away for a bit. This is outside of working out or going to a movie. This is when I can step away from the family and do whatever I want. The only rule is that it has to be something totally focused on me. So, no lawn mowing or bill paying or whatever. Sometimes I just go for a solo walk and enjoy myself. This is harder to do during the winter months, but I still take that time.

I also go to dads night out once a month. Basically, a bunch of dads and I go out for a cheap evening at a bar or a movie. This is my chance to wear my "Shannon" hat. I even make a conscious mental click when I do it because that helps with the guilt.

Yes, there's usually guilt. Or there is for some at-home dads. I'll admit I never felt guilty, because my wife is a parent, and why in the hell would I feel guilty about stepping out of her way so she can have quality time with the kids without my interference? But I know other dads (and moms) carry that guilt. Acknowledge it, accept it, and then ignore it.

Finally, now that you are starting to look after yourself and your own health, find a parenting group. These are groups that welcome any gender and are usually more accepting of the at-home dad than a mothers group. I will get into joining a dads group in a later chapter, but if you don't have one in your area, a parenting group can really help. You can find them at community centers and churches or on meetup apps. There are Tinder-like apps now built just for dads to make friends with one another. Though when you explain that to your partner, I wouldn't include the Tinder comparison if you want to stay married. That's solid advice.

## FROM THE DADS GROUP

**MICK:** I run early in the morning or late at night. Either way, when the kids are asleep, I try to take a -vantage of it. You have to take every opportunity that you can for yourself, and sometimes that means being a little tired. Is it always easy? Of course not.

**LARRY:** You have to do things for yourself and you have to do it without any guilt. Whether that is a workout, a walk, yard work, or listening to music. Whatever you enjoy, do it alone or with a friend. The important thing is to do it for you, without the kids, even if it is as simple as sitting on the porch for five to ten minutes. Carve out time every single day.

**JAKE:** I've always needed to have something for me. If I don't have that, I get angry and resentful toward whatever is preventing that. The hobby could be wood-working, video games, or even just digging deep and learning something. But I need that me time. (It's an introvert thing, Shannon wouldn't understand.)

**MIKE:** The decision for you to stay home with the kids starts and ends with you and your partner. You need to sit down and have a conversation with her and look to find time where she can take the kids and give you some time off. Because as you know, an at-home dad has no breaks. You both need to be on the same page about this. Set a regular schedule so you have something to look forward to during the week.

# GET YOUR GEAR. NOT MOM'S GEAR. YOUR GEAR.

## THE UNIFORM

There is a reason that so many fathers wear cargo shorts. Not only are we dads, we are also pack mules, and your children are amazing prospectors. They go panning through the river of life looking for those golden memories but mostly pull out snot. That snot is going to end up in your pocket one way or another.

You will accumulate crap like you are some sort of hoarder. And if a wife comes along on any adventure, then you need someplace to put her shit, too. As I am constantly reminded, most women's wear does not have pockets. A nice set of men's cargo pants offers you quadruple the storage you would normally need to make up for the shortcomings of women's fashion.

Last night I pulled out a cell phone, my wife's portable battery charger, two dryer sheets, a marble, just one M&M, three used tissues, a bolt, a small bottle of hand sanitizer, a little bit of sawdust, and Frodo's One Ring of Power. Embrace the cargo shorts. Think of them as your new uniform.

If you can, find shorts or pants made of sweat-wicking fabric. These are specially made to cool the tools down below. Your balls. I'm talking about your balls. Chafing isn't fun, and you're going to be running around enough that things are going to get moist. Now everything is gross.

## THE ADVENTURE BAG

A diaper bag is something that is designed with a stereotypical mom in mind. It's a shade of green or yellow, which matches the baby vomit on your nonstainproof shirt. It's made of leather, or faux leather, and smells like flowers. It's got a nice little pocket where you can keep your makeup. The zipper is hidden by an extra piece of fabric because for some reason zippers need to be hidden? Honestly, I have no idea. This is a diaper bag.

You are not going to carry a diaper bag. You are going to carry an adventure bag. You are not concerned about exposed zippers, and you don't need a place to keep makeup. Think of yourself as more Indiana Jones and less Nanny McPhee.

There are two basic types: the backpack and the shoulder satchel. Now, no disrespect to Dr. Jones, but I have never been a fan of the shoulder bag. It looks pretty cool when you are running from the Nazis, but there are some drawbacks.

To keep it secure, you need to loop the strap over your neck. When your toddler pulls on the adventure bag, the strap pushes right up against the carotid artery. Maybe you're into that; I don't judge. I'm just saying that passing out is not for me.

Second, the bag moves around too much, and I get nervous when heavy things are swinging at nut level. By now you know that you're probably going to get hit in the balls a lot. There is no reason to make it easier for your attackers. Having a wrecking ball swaying from your neck is just a bad idea.

For my adventure bag, I prefer to go with a backpack. It's easy to secure away from your nether regions and has plenty of exposed zippers. There is a whole industry of "fathers' gear" that has sprung up over the last several years, and they are easy enough to find. They have names like Sniper Dad Gear Camouflage Warrior's Bag. They all come in camo for some reason?

If that is something you want, then go for it. There are some really good bags. Or you can just go get a quality backpack.

Here's what you need to look for no matter what you choose:

1. Tough double stitching. You're active and your adventure bag is going to take a beating. Get something durable.

2. A small front pocket that is quickly accessible. This is where you will store your wipes and your snakebite kit if you have one. I go to weird places. The point is, wipes are your number-one need when you go out. This is something that the higher-end bags do very well, and that makes them worth it.

3. An insulated pocket. I'm going to leave the debate of formula versus breast milk to other people. I deal in reality. You need a pocket to keep bottle contents fresh no matter your choice.

4. A webbed section inside the bag where you keep only your diaper-changing supplies. Don't move them around; keep everything wrapped up together. I enjoy the webbed inner pocket because I can always quickly see what I'm missing.

5. Anything but leather.

6. Velcro. It's easier and quicker to use than a zipper. The more Velcro, the better.

## THE BABYBJÖRN / FRONT BABY CARRIER

These are great when you need both hands free. There are really just two types (although there are a thousand variations). The first type is a giant cloth wrap that looks like a curtain. Although I can appreciate the knowledge of Boy Scout knots you undoubtedly have, it's just not for me. It takes too long to get into.

> ### DAD HACK
> Don't share baby carriers with your wife. If she wants one, she needs to get her own. I know, it sounds territorial. But you're going to have to readjust the straps every time she uses it, and that's a huge pain in the ass when you have a screaming kid.

I always feel like the kid is just "kinda" in there, and how am I going to perform a tuck-and-roll with this thing? Instead, I prefer the front baby carrier, so my kid looks like Master Blaster from *Mad Max Beyond Thunderdome*. Find something with easy straps that allow for one-handed attachment and detachment. They always feel more secure to me. Do make sure it has a zippered or Velcro pocket to keep wipes for easy access. This is basically your dad saddle, you donkey. Look for many of the same things in the baby carrier as you do in the adventure bag.

## STROLLERS

There is an endless debate about strollers. Even the price range is all over the place. Fifty bucks or a thousand, your call. Here are some things to keep in mind:

1. Look for durability. When I picked out my stroller, I wanted to know that the ride was smooth and I could turn it with one hand. So make sure there are good ball bearings in the wheels. In the store, push it away from you. If it goes straight, you're off to a good start.

2. Adjustable height is an absolute must. It's a massive pain in the back if your five-foot-four wife found one that is a good size for her. This is your Batmobile, and you should treat it as such. Make sure that the cup holders fit your size of drinks, that there's a nice handy handle compartment for more wipes, and that it has a sturdy webbed bottom. This makes it easy to store your gear when your back needs a break. I used my wife's nail polish to paint flames on mine. Totally worth it.

3. Make sure it has single-handed breakdown. The best ones can collapse and lock with a twist of your wrist and are light enough that you can load it into the car without killing yourself. When you pick out your stroller, do some curls with it. It's something to think about because you will never have both hands free. Ever.

4. Form follows function. Bigger tires if you are planning on doing a lot of off-road stroller hiking. I did a ton of this, and it shows on my stroller. The thing is wrecked and beautiful. Jogging strollers for the runners, midsize

strollers for the stores, a beast for the adventures. Sit-and-stand strollers work wonderfully for those with a baby and a toddler.

## THERMOS OR INSULATED CUP

You're going to need coffee. Get a cup that has a secure lid, can be closed off, and keeps things hot for a LONG time. Find one that fits in your adventure bag or your stroller. I'll admit, I don't like coffee. But I love hot chocolate that I can pretend is coffee. I fit in with the other dads, who turned out to be coffee snobs. I'm looking at you, Jake.

## CAR GEAR

This is often overlooked but is equally as important as everything else mentioned. A **rear-facing mirror** that reflects your baby's face is great. Is the baby almost asleep? Do I need to keep driving around? Also, invest in a **pocketed car organizer** that hangs off the back of your seat. Use this to keep extra supplies and an emergency pacifier. I know that not everyone uses the pacifier. I also know that those people break when they're on a five-hour car trip and a pacifier would save their sanity. Finally, get a **special small car bag** containing the extra essentials that may be needed. There are days when you walk out of the house and you thought you had an extra onesie only to discover that it was really your oil rag from the garage.

## SOFT-SIDED COOLER

This is something that my dads group uses a ton. I go through these things so quickly just from overuse. We do a lot of picnics at the park, and sometimes we keep our worms in there when I take the kids fishing. Rule of thumb: get something that's big enough for a six-pack but still fits in the bottom of the stroller. Soft sides save your legs, but having a hard plastic interior will make it easier to clean and prevent leakage. We will get to building a budget later, but the picnic lunch that can be had no matter where you are saves a ton of money. I've had whole days full of museums and lunches without spending a dime. This is one of the reasons why.

**NOW YOU ARE** all Ramboed up. It's time to head out into the world or the Communists win.

> ### Because Dad Says So . . .
>
> *Swaddlers are specially designed sleeping blankets that wrap around the baby. It is something that helps the baby self-soothe in order to be able to fall asleep, which makes life a lot easier on Dad!*
>
> **Robb Tavill, father of two**

## FROM THE DADS GROUP

**MICK:** If you're going with the jogging stroller, get one that has a lockable front wheel. You want that front wheel locked in place because if you don't, it will get so bumpy a baby is going to go flying. But it can double as a normal stroller for daily adventures once the wheel is unlocked. This is a lot more versatile and will save you some money.

**LARRY:** With a cooler, the longer the ice lasts, the better. Some say the ice lasts, but they lie. Get something soft-sided, leakproof, and with a comfortable strap. Check around with your friends and online, whatever, but do your research. Velcro pockets are nice, as well as a small hand port to grab what you need without opening the entire lid.

**JAKE:** The best gear is different for everyone, but when you do find something important to you, don't be afraid to buy the nice version of it. Yes, it costs more, but you use it every day and you use it hard. Spending more really does get you a better product sometimes.

**MIKE:** Dude, not every outing requires a complete kit of crap to haul around. A couple of diapers in your cargo pants, wipes in the back pocket, and a few extra things here and there and you can get out the door in under five minutes.

# HEAD OUT INTO THE WORLD. WELCOME TO THE LAND OF OZ, WHERE YOU'RE NOT SURE OF THE RULES, THERE IS NO PATH TO FOLLOW, AND SOME CRAZY LADY KEEPS YELLING AT YOU.

Ninety percent of your interactions with other parents are going to be all peaches and cream. It's going to be normal with people just trying to be people. It's just like playing a nice game of Chutes and Ladders. Everything is sweet and smells like candy canes at Christmas.

But then halfway through you realize it isn't Chutes and Ladders at all. It's Risk, and some jerk has built up on Australia and you're about to get steamrolled.

That's the problem with being a guy in the at-home parenting world. Sometimes you don't even understand what game you are playing.

Here's what you need to know.

## DAD HACK

Clip a couple of mountaineer carabiners to your bag. They are handy as hell and easy to work with one hand. It's where I keep an extra stuffed toy if I need it. Just clip it through the tag and you are ready for any meltdown. And if the situation presents itself, you can climb Mount Everest.

## PACK LIKE YOU MEAN IT

I'll admit that, in the beginning, I didn't really know what to pack in my adventure bag. I had sandpaper in there at one point. Even after all these years, I have no idea why. I cringe at young me. Besides sandpaper, here is what to keep in your adventure bag:

1. Diapers.
2. Wipes.
3. Butt cream.
4. Extra clothes. At least two onesies for a baby. For a toddler, more underwear than shirts.
5. Snacks of your choice for both the kid and you.
6. Two bottles and nipples.
7. Formula. If you're using breast milk, it's still nice to have some on hand in case shit goes sideways.
8. Water in either a thermos or your insulated pouch. Temperature is dependent on whether you are formula feeding or using breast milk.
9. Sunscreen and a hat depending on the weather.
10. Some sort of hand sanitizer, because those little buttholes touch everything.
11. Extra pacifier, if used.
12. Burp cloth, because sometimes the wipes just aren't enough.
13. A changing pad.
14. A stuffed toy or teething ring, whatever your kid is into.

## Because Dad Says So . . .

*Keep Post-it notes in your bag. They are great for covering automatic flush toilets that scare some kids who are potty training.*

**Mike Flynn, father of two**

Those are the basics of what should be in your adventure bag. Keep in mind that you are Dad, you will always be Dad, and you are not trying to be Mom. Therefore, do not shy away from putting some "extra" things in your bag. For example, I keep duct tape in my bag and have for years. When the adhesive tag on your last diaper breaks off, it's handy to have the tape around. I have also used it to repair all the toys my kids have broken.

## THE MOMS

You want to know what it's really like to interact with the at-home moms. What can you expect? How do you approach the moms and ask for their number for a playdate without sounding super creepy?

Well, for starters, ask for emails before numbers. And second, it really depends on what type of mom you are dealing with.

### The Good Witch Glinda Mom

- Treats you like a normal parent, not a predator.
- Tends to include you in conversations and makes it a point to ask about your kids.
- Great to learn from.

- Realizes that you're both on the same path and therefore share a common bond.
- Magical and awesome and their eyes sparkle with the beauty of their overpowering aura.

How to approach:

- "Hi, I'm Dad. May I give you a high five?" Parents love high fives. Most of your interactions with the moms will be of this variety.

### The Whatever Mom

- After the Good Witch Glinda, the second-most-common mom.
- Scientifically proven to be unable to see you. As a dad, you are invisible to them. I was once sat on by one of these moms. Like, really sat on. My arm was on a bench and she just sat on me. Plopped right down. I'll tell you the story later in Chapter 3, but I want to put it here to prove a point. Not cool, man. Not cool.
- Notices her kids but just barely more than she notices you.
- Commonly found at story hour, sing-alongs, and the mall.
- Has a husband that she loves but . . . or so I hear, because when someone sits on you, you are ethically cleared to listen in on their conversations.

How to approach:

- With a large swing band that rides in on a train while fireworks go off. They still won't notice you, but that's always a cool way to walk into a room. Seriously, it's a bit freaky how much you DON'T get noticed by these moms. But start with your best dad joke. I wish you the best of luck.

## The Mary Poppins Mom

- Absolutely perfect in every way.
- Carries a magical bag that has an endless supply of baby gear she's willing to share.
- Not a hair out of place. Never wears sweatpants. I saw one of these fine moms pushing a stroller up a mountain in high heels. It was fucking impressive. A mountain. Seriously.
- Kind and helpful. Gives absolutely great advice that you should always listen to.
- A little judgmental, but in a polite kind of way.
- Enjoys new friendships, great for conversation.

How to approach:
- With a recommendation from Mr. Banks or just introduce yourself politely. These are some of my favorite moms, but on some level, seeing how competent they are reminds me of how inadequate I can be.

## The Instagram Mom

- Looks and acts like the Mary Poppins Mom, but it's all for show.
- There is no depth; she doesn't want a conversation with you unless you can craft cupcakes out of non-GMO organic grass-fed wheat.
- Often carries around name-brand coffee in cutesy photogenic coffee mugs. Stops often to take pictures.

- Excellent photography. If you meet one of these, she should handle any group shots.
- Quick to dismiss you once it is discovered that you have a small social media following.

How to approach:
- Exchange Instagram handles and obsessively "like" every social media post she makes.

### The Yeller Mom

- Can easily be spotted when she screams, "WHY ARE YOU AT THE PARK WHERE THERE ARE CHILDREN AROUND OH MY GOD SOMEONE THINK OF THE CHILDREN THERE ARE CHILDREN HERE!"
- Extra-supernova maternal, as in there is no way a man could ever want to care for children in the way she cares for children. You can't understand because you're not a maternal mother.
- Cusses and then denies that she cusses. A unique trait to this particular brand of mom.
- Will not laugh when she sees a dad call himself a motherfucker, even though that is one of the best dirty dad jokes ever.
- After your joke, she is going to accuse you of the Lindbergh kidnapping.
- Loves making a righteous scene. She's probably going to call the cops.
- Expects you to apologize once she is proven wrong.

How to approach:
- You don't; she approaches you.

### The Wolf-Pack Mom
- Extremely territorial. Likes to pee on trees.
- These moms travel in tight groups and quickly lay all their gear on any good seats left, even though they aren't using them. Get used to sitting on the floor, bucko. Like the movie *Mean Girls* but with more side-eye.
- Treats other moms not in the alpha pack the exact way that she treats you.
- Wears capri pants.
- Should you attempt conversation, you will immediately be seen as trying to hit on her.
- If you do get in with this particular mom, it's kinda awesome to be part of the badasses. It feels very safe for some reason.

How to approach:
- Do not make direct eye contact. Make sure that your belly is exposed as you offer her a raw espresso.

### The "How Dare You!" Mom
- Will read the above list and get super pissed that we (you and I are in it together now, buddy!) used stereotypes to poke fun at 50 percent of the parenting population.
- Will say, "Why can't you do this with dads?" and has a point. There is the Dad Bro, the Barbecue Dad, the Over-the-Top Dad (that's me), the Deadbeat Dad (fuck that guy), and the Craft-Beer-Dad-Whose-Beer-Still-Tastes-Like-Shit Dad.

- Even though you have included a joke making fun of dads, she will still be upset enough to ask for your manager so she can complain.

How to approach:
- Quickly and without remorse, sacrifice all of your dad friends to the mom so that you can make an escape. All hate mail can be sent directly to Larry.

That's the moms in a nutshell. That was all really just a funny way of saying you'll meet all types. The same dicks that are at your workplace are now at the park. But the same awesome people are, too. To start a conversation, ask for their advice when you see something that impresses you. All parents love to give advice, and some of them eventually write books for other parents. Really do keep a dad joke handy as an icebreaker. Here is an oldie but a goodie: When does a joke become a dad joke? When it becomes apparent. Wocka wocka. General rules: be clean, be polite, and just treat people the way you want to be treated.

Let's go over some of the other situations you will commonly face as an at-home dad.

## Because Dad Says So . . .

*I always put "keep the kids alive" at the top of my to-do list. That way, even if I accomplish nothing else, I can still cross one thing off the list. And if I fail at that one thing, I just change it to "keep MOST OF the kids alive." It's okay to move the goalposts.*

**James Breakwell, father of four, author of Bare Minimum**

Parenting: Not Quite Ruining Your Child *and* Only Dead on
the Inside: A Parent's Guide to Surviving the Zombie
Apocalypse

## ˙ARE YOU BABYSITTING?˙

You're going to get this question a lot. It's usually from a nice
grandma or the receptionist at the doctor's office. If it's not this
one, it's, "Are you giving Mom a break today?"

I know some dads who get pretty huffy about these questions.
Believe me, I understand the feeling. Once you've heard it a thousand times, it becomes a bit insulting. Realize that when it's said,
it's not meant with any ill intent. Most times, I just shrug it off
or tell people that I'm an at-home dad. Sometimes I say I'm a
motherfucking dad, but that joke doesn't work as well in a grocery
store.

The National At-Home Dad Network (athomedad.org) rep-
resents stay-at-home dads and actually makes a T-shirt that
proudly proclaims DADS DON'T BABYSIT. I recommend getting a
T-shirt, as it will save you a lot of chitchat.

## THE ONLY DAD THERE

You are an island in a sea of moms. When I go to story hour and
sit on the floor, it's like I'm protected by an invisible moat. On the
plus side, I do enjoy the extra legroom. But I also acknowledge
the fact that I'm a big dude with a beard, and that can put people off.

Embrace the awkwardness of being the only dad there. There
is no helping it. If you're comfortable with yourself and what you

now do for a living, honestly this won't bother you much. Don't change anything about how you act; just be you, because you are pretty fucking awesome. With any luck, the joint will be filled with Good Witch Glindas or Mary Poppinses.

## THE DOOR-TO-DOOR SALESMAN

Holy crap, these guys. You know what, Dads? Take a break. Let me talk to the Door-to-Door Salesman for you. I've got your back on this one.

Ahem.

You motherfucking slimy nap-ruining piece of shit. You saw the sign above the doorbell that read BABY NAPPING! DO NOT RING! You rang that shit anyway. What the ever-loving fuckity fuck is fucking wrong with you?

Do you know what happens when you ring that thing, you turd-swallowing dumpster heap? The baby wakes up and the baby is mad. And do you know who he gets mad at? Not you, lord fucking forbid, no. He gets mad at me. Then he wakes his sister up and she gets mad at me. Pretty soon, everyone is screaming because you had to ignore the huge fucking sign.

So pack up your little case of carpet swatches, and stick it right up your ass. Because I've got bigger things to deal with, like two kids who are going all *Lord of the Flies* in here.

God, that felt good.

All right, Dads, let me talk to you again. This is an advice book, after all, so do you know what you do when this syphilitic potato shows up during nap time, ignores the fucking sign, and wakes the kids up?

You invite him right the fuck in. Yup, come on in, good sir who wants to pillage my medicine cabinet for expired oxy.

Sit his ass down, go get the kids, and hand them right to him. Watch his face fall when he doesn't know what to do. Sit back and listen to his screams as he begins to rethink his life choices.

He'll be trying hard to protect his throat as your toddler remembers her preschool ninja training. Take one Goldfish cracker and throw it at his face when he starts to lose hope. The children will rip him apart to get the last good thing left in the house.

FedEx or UPS guys, this doesn't apply to you. You never ring the doorbell when I'm home. EVER. Even when you creepily looked through my side window and caught me dancing in my underwear. We made eye contact. I know you saw me.

I need a drink.

## FROM THE DADS GROUP

**MICK:** I get the "Are you babysitting?" thing a lot. Most times, I let it go. Does it get exhausting? Yeah. I would say to the new guys, correct it when it really matters, like at the preschool or the doctor's office. Make sure that they know you are the primary caregiver because if you don't, they'll always call Mom first. Mom is at the office. Call me. That's a pain in the butt.

**LARRY:** There are lots of different moms groups out there. One is not going to be like another. So, if you have one bad experience, don't put it on all of them. Talk with the moms at the park where your kids are playing. Invite them back for another day if the kids are playing really well together.

**JAKE:** Door-to-door salesmen wake sleeping children. I know they are going to a special circle of hell.*

**MIKE:** Don't stress about being the only dad at any specific place. Focus on your kids and you'll be fine. If there is another dad there, give him the traditional head nod and start up a conversation.

---

* Author's note: Jake wouldn't discuss this any further and honestly, it got a bit scary, so I stopped asking.

# CHAPTER 2

# SURVIVING THE GRIND

Day in and day out, parenting isn't easy. You're tired and dirty and might end up losing a toe.

## WORDS OF WISDOM

My life as a stay-at-home dad was a vaudeville act at times. Focus on the privilege and joy in spending time with your kids. Find creative ways to make parenting fun and entertaining. The humor, comedy, goofiness, and laughter that filled our day surpassed the daily grind of being a parent.

**Hogan Hilling, father of three**

Let's not sugarcoat any of this: parenting is fucking hard. For you, the new at-home dad, parenting has just been taken up a notch. Being an at-home dad means that you get no sick leave and no vacation days and that someone is going to hit you in the balls.

Parenting can be very boring when you do the same thing every day. The monotony is tough to handle, especially when the kids are young. You may feel limited and stuck in a rut. The same cartoons, the same activities, the same thing every day.

Add the constant interruptions when you finally manage to get something accomplished, and it just gets harder. Regardless of your kid's age, this happens all the time. For example, as I write this right now, my seven-year-old, Oliver, decided it was a good time to jump on my head, Vivi got the mail key stuck in the mailbox, and Wyatt needed me to take out my headphones to ask me what was for dinner. It's not even noon. All of that happened in the time it took to write one paragraph. I would like to say that it's worse when they are younger. It is not. It's about the same. There are interruptions interrupting your interruptions.

Let's dispel a few myths right from the get-go that people have of stay-at-home parents. Obviously, we have copious amounts of free time during the day to work on cutesy little side projects and have butterfly parties. Making dinner every day isn't that hard. Cleaning is enjoyable. Surely, most days at-home parents sit on the couch while reading the latest bestseller.

What a load of shit.

My first month as an at-home dad was done 100 percent on my own. It was a trial by puke. For some dumbass reason, my wife and I decided to move across the country during my first month as the primary caregiver. Erin accepted a better-paying job three states away. In fact, this was one of the catalysts that led to our decision. We were going to start fresh in a new town and with a new system! Vivi was less than two, Wyatt was a newborn, and Oliver wasn't even a thought.

On day one, my wife left for our new town. My job was to take care of the two kids, sell our house, pack our belongings, organize a daily schedule, and provide a clean and loving learning environment. There were also two cats and two dogs.

That shit plan lasted four days before I broke.

Vivi got sick and puked all over my face. Literally, in my face while I was sitting on the couch. I was exhausted. Wyatt wasn't even sleeping through the night, and as you've heard, I couldn't even shower with a shower curtain. At one point, I found myself sitting on the edge of the bathtub holding my daughter with her head over my shoulder as she went all *Exorcist* with projectile vomit, rocking my son in his car seat with my foot so he would stop screaming, and watching my dog lick vomit off the baby. I was completely covered in puke. It was in my chest hair and ran down my back to the crack of my ass.

That is what the grind of parenting is like. It's not glamorous and it's never easy. Because if something is suddenly easy, that means your house is getting destroyed. Even when you think you've got a moment to yourself, the anxiety comes crashing in as a terrible defense mechanism.

I wouldn't wish my first thirty days on anyone. However, on a positive note, doing it like that makes you become self-reliant real fucking quick. I had to keep the house spotless for prospective buyers, which meant I had to learn new strategies and find easier ways to do things. I had to cook three meals a day while barely being able to stand. I had to sign the contracts when the house actually sold. I did that with both kids on my lap and the contract being colored on with a purple crayon.

By the time we moved, at the very least I had a handle on a couple of truths. First, this is way, way harder than I thought it would be, and there is no backup. And second, as an at-home parent, you are the cavalry. You are the help. You are the guy who everyone looks to when things go wrong. All that weight is always on your shoulders. It grinds you down.

Make no mistake, I have fucked up so many times that it would take another book just to give you my highlights. You will, too, but from our failures we learn. You'll figure out that there are easier ways to do things, that you don't have to be perfect, and that you got this.

Hopefully, you can learn from my mistakes to mitigate your own. And when you do fuck up, just know that I've done way worse. I was asked to leave a football stadium because the kids were being too loud. When you can top that one, we'll talk.

Let's begin by getting you through the grind of day-to-day parenting.

## START WITH A STRONG FOUNDATION

Before you lift a finger, you've got to figure out some things. This isn't the type of job that you can run into with a good battle cry and hope that things work out. I tried that and took a face full of vomit. As impressive as my battle cry is and as much as I've enjoyed teaching it to my kids, it doesn't really do anything other than make me feel cool.

This is going to be a running theme in this chapter: Start with a strong foundation. Don't start with the battle cry, start with the battle plan. Having a plan in place, even if it's just an overall abstract, is going to make life easier. This is the first step to surviving everything that comes next.

Let's make a plan.

# GET YOUR JOB DESCRIPTION IN WRITING

You need to set expectations for both you and your significant other. I'm not even remotely kidding. This is where a lot of guys fail at the beginning.

"Oh, my wife and I talked about this. We're good." You know what? Go chase those dreams for a month and let me know how it works out. When you can't stop arguing with your partner and your kid has joined a toddler biker gang, come back and I'll take care of you.

How specific did you get? Unless you got a point-by-point description, it's not specific enough. I mean down to each and every chore or responsibility you will have. What is the cleaning schedule, what will be cleaned, what time is dinner, what happens if dinner isn't available? Those are the kinds of the specific questions you need to answer.

Do you get time off and, if so, what does that look like? How does that work? What about your spouse, do they get time off? Did you talk about your mental health and what to do to make that a priority? And none of this happens in a vacuum, so what's the impact going to be on your partner during your time at home? Are you going to cook dinner every night, or are they going to do a meal on the weekend? What are you going to do when you get sick?

You are doing all this to prevent future arguments. You can't wing it here.

Right at the beginning, you are setting up expectations. A big question that I get from new guys who came to our group is usually related to "the talk" not really being a talk. The spouse feels that the at-home dad is not doing enough, and the dad feels that he is doing everything. Nowhere does this come up as much as it does with cleaning.

Everyone has different levels of clean. For example, my wife hates the way I vacuum. I hate the way she doesn't vacuum. There needs to be an understanding of what each person thinks of as clean, because with children it's hard to get to that point. I don't hang up my wife's shirts because those things are not meant to be hung up without a degree in engineering. I fold everything and put it in a basket, and she takes it from there.

For my wife's part, she usually handles Sunday night dinner and does much of the bedtime routine. This gives me a break while she gets that all-important one-on-one time with the kids. This didn't happen magically or organically. It took hard discussions and some uncomfortable arguments to find the middle ground that worked for us.

This is why you get a detailed, point-by-point job description before you even start staying at home. Think of it this way: When you start a new job, you are given a list of job responsibilities and duties. This job is no different.

## ESTABLISH A ROUTINE

Routine is both your savior and your jailer. A routine can be so monotonous that you'll welcome a kick in the face just to stay awake. However, a routine helps the children know what to expect and gives them a sense of control and security. That kind of structure makes things easier. Again, you're managing expectations.

However, doing the same thing day in and day out is very, very boring. The load is tougher mentally than it is physically.

The trick is learning to bend the routine enough to hold your own interest without changing it too much so that the kids still have that sense of security.

I'm going to give you my own routine that I used for years. Change what you need to, but this gives you at least a starting place. You'll see where this schedule allows me flexibility to change it up every week. Each of the dads in my group has a routine that has similarities but is different enough that it works for them. Some are more rigid than others.

**MONDAY:** Short workout and grocery shopping in the morning. Lunch and naps, and an afternoon filled with the library, the park, or playtime at home. During naps I tackled the bigger cleaning items on my list, such as dusting or repair work. At four p.m. we did a quick cleanup of the first two rooms my wife would walk into when she got home. This would create a good impression so our night could start off on a good note. This didn't happen every time, of course, but the four o'clock cleanup has since become a habit that we still continue. Then I started dinner at five.

**TUESDAY:** Adventure day for me and the kids. From eight to twelve, we explored the city or countryside. Some days the other dads would come. We called these days Rebel Tuesdays. A picnic lunch if the weather was nice, then home for naps, cleaning, and chores. The rest of the day looked like Monday.

WEDNESDAY: Work out at the gym in the morning then off to
playgroup. Naps on the ride home, and if I was
lucky, I could carry them still asleep to their beds.
Or I just sat in my car in the driveway while they
slept. Every parent has done that. There is no
shame. Then it was back to our Monday schedule.

THURSDAY: Deep-clean day. This isn't the quick pickup or
cleanup while I move. This is the deep stuff that
needs to get done, like cleaning bathrooms,
washing sheets, etc. I wanted to have a clean
home for the weekend with my wife. Although I
would certainty clean a lot during the week, this
day was completely devoted to the task. Some
guys space this out, but I found it more
beneficial to get it all done in one day. Now,
cleaning with kids is tough. The whole next
section is devoted to it. Early on, I would have to
strap Vivi to my chest in her BabyBjörn as I
vacuumed. As they grew, they helped with tasks
they could complete. Most days, they just threw
crap everywhere so it was like I had to do the
same task twice. Eventually, I just gave my son a
broom and hoped his toddler self would
accidently sweep a floor. He mostly hit his sister.

FRIDAY: Adventure day with the other dads. Lunch out
on a picnic or at someplace cheap. Even in
restaurants, the kids would bring a lunch
because for some odd reason they didn't like
barbecue. It is my failure as a father. Then home
for naps, following the same pattern as Monday.

SATURDAY Family time with the wife, but naps still occurred
& SUNDAY: at one, sticking to the nap schedule. I wanted to
keep the weekend days as free of chores as I
possibly could. This was our time to bond as a
family without the stress of fixing things. It
doesn't always work, as there are times when I
needed to do repair work around the house that I
couldn't when the kids were with me. With that
said, you need to recognize that time together as
a family is important. Not just for you, but for
your spouse and kids.

Looking over the routine, you can see where I kept it flexible.
On Tuesdays and Fridays, I was never home before nap time.
This allowed the kids and me to explore in the mornings, and it
kept me mentally alert. Things changed enough on those days
that I was always excited. My general rule: If you aren't home,
then you can't make a mess. And getting out of the house every
day, even if just for a short walk, is fucking essential.

## FROM THE DADS GROUP

**MICK:** Talk to your wife. Establish a routine.

**LARRY:** Talk to your wife. Establish a routine.

**JAKE:** Talk to your wife. Establish a routine.

**MIKE:** Talk to Shannon's wife. Then talk to your wife.
Establish a routine.

# THE ART OF CLEANING WITH CHILDREN

If your wife bought you this book, this section is probably why. The problem with cleaning while parenting is that you have to clean while parenting. It's a catch-22. Some days, you'll clean all day and the house will still look like shit. Inform your spouse that it's going to happen.

It's in the prep work that you'll find your success. This is something we all eventually figure out. A word of caution here. There is no hack, tip, or magic spell that will make cleaning the toilet easier. That's not a thing. The actual cleaning has to get done, one way or another. What we more experienced parents have figured out is the more prepared you are, the easier it will be. This is the industry standard for us at-home parents. Let's keep it simple.

### Because Dad Says So . . .

*One fun thing about kids is they love to "help" with household tasks like putting sheets on beds. Unfortunately, they're terrible at it. So the best plan is to sneak away while they're distracted to get the job done yourself. And when that inevitably fails and they catch you in the act, just cut your losses and give up. Don't put any sheets on beds for five to ten years. Simple.*

**Andrew Knott, father of three**

1. **Declutter.** If you aren't using it, store it or get rid of it. If you are not sure, use the three-box method. The first box is for things you wish to keep, the second box is for things to throw away, and the third box is for anything you're not sure about. Store the third box for a month. If you haven't gone back to that box in that time, consider getting rid of the contents.

2. **How hard is that new thing to clean?** This is the question you need to ask before you bring anything into the house. My mother-in-law once got my daughter a dry-clean-only comforter. That was some bullshit. When looking at new furniture, is the fabric going to be ruined with a stain? Are the curtains easy to wash? Simple and easy is always better.

3. **Get organized.** Put baskets in every room for a quick storage place during the day for life's knickknacks. Empty them at the end of the day. Keep baby wipes in all areas that often need a quick wipe down. Look at all your shelf space and bins and decide if you have enough.

4. **Tech.** Look into the apps Unfilth Your Habitat and Tody to keep yourself on task with the cleaning. If you don't have a smart-home device, like Google Home or Amazon Echo, consider getting one. They're great for maintaining the calendar, ordering supplies, and finding quick recipes. *Good Housekeeping* has a skill on the Amazon Echo that alphabetically lists all carpet stains and gives you instructions on how to clean them.

5. **Baking soda and vinegar.** Get familiar with them as cleaning products. There's an entire genre of writing dedicated to these two household supplies. In general,

baking soda acts as an abrasive and vinegar is your degreaser and germ killer. They can also be used to treat carpet stains. Both can be used to soak up odors. There are 1,001 uses for baking soda and vinegar.

> **DAD HACK**
> Stinky dishwasher or washing machine?
> Washing machine: Mix ¼ cup of baking soda into a cup of hot tap water and pour into empty washing machine. Add 1 cup of vinegar. Run cycle on hot.
> Dishwasher: Sprinkle 1 cup of baking soda on bottom of dishwasher. Add 2 cups of vinegar. Run empty cycle on hot. Clean filters in soapy water afterward.

6. **Strategically placed cleaning supplies.** Keep supplies safely stored where you use them to prevent having to run around gathering everything. For example, store supplies in both upstairs and downstairs bathrooms. With kids around, you'll have both hands full and it helps to not have to search for cleaning supplies.

7. **Educate yourself.** Like I said, cleaning is its own genre, so take the time to go to the library and read up. Get the books that work for you. Knowing is half the battle. (Thanks, G.I. Joe.) There is something called Swedish death cleaning. I like it just for the name.

Get these things done at the beginning, and you're on your way to being able to clean the house with kids around.

## CLEANING STRATEGIES

There is no right way or wrong way to clean unless you have OCD, in which case this part is probably a breeze for you. If you don't, here are some common strategies that will make it easier to clean with children. And, as always, start with a routine.

1. **Establish a routine.** You have a weekly routine; now do it on the daily for cleaning. As you clean, keep the same process. As the kids grow, they'll know what to expect and what their jobs are.

2. **Clean from the top down.** Shit rolls downhill and so does dust. Start dusting at the top and work your way to the floor. Clean the upstairs before the downstairs. Paint ceilings before floors. You get the idea.

3. **Put the kids to work.** Kids love putting things in things. That's why you have baskets. Give the kids daily chores as soon as they are able. Putting toys away, putting laundry in baskets, or even throwing away trash is going to save you time and energy. A two-year-old is fantastic at putting wet clothes into the dryer. Make sure they don't climb in, though. That's bad.

### Because Dad Says So . . .

*As your kids grow, give them an area of responsibility. This is their domain to maintain and clean. You'll get better results when they are part of the solution.*

**Curtis Webster Jr., father of three**

4. **Do laundry.** At least one load a day. There is no escaping the laundry apocalypse. Accept your fate.

5. **Keep toys out of the main living areas.** No one wants to curb stomp on a Lego. That's a good way to lose a foot. There has to be at least one room that isn't controlled by toys. Keep it clutter-free and a respite for you and your spouse.

6. **Clean as you go.** You're going to be walking all day. Sitting down is not possible. As you pass by something on the floor or counter that doesn't belong there but does belong in the room you're going to, pick it up and take it with you. You can clean an entire house like this in a day.

7. **Leave one room messy.** Allow one room to be less than perfect. It's okay. Clean it more weekly than daily. Do a pick up every once in a while, but just know that it's okay if this room isn't sparkling. For most of us, it's the kids' toy room.

8. **Complete the four o'clock cleanup.** Every day, without fail, my kids and I do this. It gets the house presentable before my wife comes home and allows me to put away everything that is in baskets. The kids expect it and do their chores without being asked. On those days that the house is wrecked and you can't clean, focus on the first two rooms that your spouse will see when they walk in the door. Get those done first. This good first impression gives them a sense of calm and sets the right tone for the evening. This is how you maintain on those off-the-rails days.

9. **Utilize baby carriers and playpens.** I love baby jail. The young ones can't be out of sight or help you scrub the oven, so the playpen lets you keep an eye on them. When

I vacuumed, I often put the baby in a carrier and just made an activity out of it. And yes, sometimes my son rode on the vacuum like a horse because that's cool.

10. **Know that sometimes nothing works.** Some days, cleaning is just not going to happen. The living room has food on the carpet, the toy room is a hazard area, and the table has so much glitter on it that it looks like Tinker Bell threw a party. On those days, throw up your hands and be okay with it. If you've had the proper talk with the spouse beforehand, it will be okay. Don't make it a habit, though.

There's a lot more advice out there. People have made whole careers discussing how to clean with kids around. Look at the website cleanmama.com. It does a wonderful job of breaking down every routine, chore, or area when it comes to cleaning.

## DAD IT UP

All cleaning products are gender biased. There, I said it. None of the cleaning sprays, products, or gear is made with Dad in mind. I have yet to find a pair of cleaning gloves that fit my gorilla hands. One size fits all, my ass.

Once you realize that, your job is to pick products and equipment that actually make the job easier. We are not confined to what is marketed. That's your superpower. It's the power of Dad and getting shit done. Add these to your cleaning supplies, and you can thank me later.

- **Wet/dry vac.** Most people laugh when I tell them that I had one in my dining room for years and years. They think it's funny until they remember how kids eat. Nothing stays on the table. Do this for six months and you'll see the wisdom of the wet/dry vacuum. The nozzle is huge and will literally suck up everything. It's not that I don't use my regular vacuum, but I save Little Carol for the more delicate jobs. For the big spills, the beast comes out. A two-year-old loves the wet/dry vac. Watch what they stuff up there, though. It can take off Barbie's wig. By the age of three, Vivi would get the wet/dry vac out by herself when she finished a meal. Of course, I think she made a bigger mess once she discovered how fun it was to throw food in the nozzle. Still worth it.

- 8" × 10" tarp. If you are potty training, get the tarp out. How is this not an industry standard? Seriously? It's common sense. I'm just saying it's easier to clean pee off a tarp than it is to clean it off the carpet. Potty training is a piss fest and your toddler is the main attraction.

### DAD HACK

To clean pee off the carpet, blot with a solution of 50 percent vinegar and 50 percent water. Blot, don't scrub, until pee is removed. For more robust human poop stains, start with the vinegar-water solution. If stain persists, apply hydrogen peroxide directly to the stain. Hydrogen peroxide also works well to remove blood, chocolate, and wine stains. Whatever you use, always test first on a small patch of carpet that is out of the way, in case the solution discolors your carpet.

- WD-40, utility knife, and blunt-edge scraper. Put these three things with your cleaning supplies. WD-40 gets gum out of

hair and marker off walls. The utility knife is for tape and stickers that kids put everywhere. A blunt-edge scraper is for when you need a softer touch on flooring.
- **Long-handled dustpan.** You've seen these at restaurants. That's what you run now. Your back will be very appreciative.

## DOLLAR-STORE CLEANERS VERSUS EXPENSIVE CLEANERS

There is a great debate between my dads group and me about whether you should buy your cleaning products at the dollar store.

I am a big believer that it is just fine to buy your sprays, washes, and mops at a very discounted price. Why would I go to some big-box retailer and spend twelve times the price for something that smells the same? I would rather help my budget out, which is important, and instead buy five quality cleaning products for five bucks. This also leaves room for the purchase of a candy bar.

My dads group happens to disagree with me, but that is mainly because they are colossal buttholes. It is clear to me that they have fallen into the pocket of the big cleaning companies and are paid shills. And we all know that Big Cleaning is a gateway into Big Pharma.

Mick and Larry claim that if you clean with dollar products, then your house will "look like it's cleaned by dollar products." I think it's fair to concede that fact, but I will once again rely on my counterpoint of being able to buy a candy bar.

## DAD HACK

Homemade cleaner: It's the same as your beginner carpet cleaner. Mix 50 percent vinegar with 50 percent water. But this time, add a couple of drops of a manly essential oil such as cedarwood. This will be the only time in this entire book that I tell you it's okay to use essential oils. Safety tip because it has to be said: Never mix bleach and ammonia. That's how you die, so don't do it.

## FROM THE DADS GROUP

**MICK:** Pick a paint with medium to high gloss and good durability. The hardware store will help you pick it out. You need something that can constantly be scrubbed and not peel away.

**LARRY:** To clean your grill, after every use, scrub the grates with the grill brush and then coat them with grape-seed oil. This protects from rust and removes any grease. Cover and store when complete.

**JAKE:** Pay attention to places that accumulate water. Your bathrooms, kitchens, etc. Keep things dry, so no standing water. If you do notice mold and it's only on the surface, you can kill and remove it with bleach. Then use a fan to quickly dry the area. If the mold is in the object itself, such as a wall, then you have to replace it.

**MIKE:** You don't have to clean everything all at the same time. Break it down into smaller jobs and smaller sections that are more manageable. Do this in spurts while the kids are occupied. Clean as you go about your day. That way, you maintain a level of clean throughout the whole week. There's absolutely no need to try to have your home spotless all the time, and you'll drive yourself crazy trying to keep up.

## COOKING AND MEAL PREP IN THE EYE OF THE TORNADO

The first step in becoming a top-notch chef is to pick a proper name. Something with grandeur and a bit of intrigue. Bonus points if it sounds French. To come up with your chef moniker, combine the name of your first pet and the street you grew up on. I am Coco Paintbrush. Let's hit the kitchen.

I don't know if you're a Julia Child in the kitchen or more of a glue eater. Maybe you're already a great cook and can make that steak au poivre just right every single time. But let me ask you: Have you ever done it while getting punched in the balls?

It's not that the cooking is especially hard; it's that you have to do it 1,095 times a year. I did the math. That's a lot of cooking. Let's be generous and assume that someone else is going to cook a meal a few times a year. That's still 1,092 meals.

You're less of an artist here and more of a short-order cook with a diner full of foulmouthed little bastards that are not shy about sharing their opinions. To top it all off, you have to create every meal while being constantly interrupted and sometimes assaulted.

Let's start with some basics. If you don't know how to cook, fire up YouTube or head to your local library. There are so many books, videos, and grandma tips out there that you can teach yourself. But I would HIGHLY recommend starting with *America's Test Kitchen Family Cookbook, 3rd Edition*. With this cookbook you'll start out simple (how to boil an egg) and end with some true masterpieces, such as seared chicken and braised fennel with a white wine and Parmesan sauce. By the time you are finished with that book, you'll know that steak au poivre is just a fancy French name for peppered steak with butter sauce.

## NUTRITION AND MEAL PLANNING

Not every one of those 1,092 meals are going to be an organic health fest, because some days I need a damn hamburger. On the whole, though, you need to understand the nutritional value of food and learn to read labels. Your job is to raise a healthy family, not a butter-eating supervillain.

Do your research, but the general advice is to stock up on fresh fruits and vegetables, especially during snack times. For kids, prepare snacks and meals that are low in sugar, and for adults, watch the carbs and sodium intake.

### Because Dad Says So . . .

*The common trap that dads fall into is eating when and what the kids have, but they have different metabolisms than us and get more healthy motion during the day. Ideally, we should fuel our body six times a day, with three healthy meals (low in carbs, fat, sugar, and sodium) as well as three healthy snacks (think almonds, fresh fruit/ veggies). Eating at regular intervals helps keep our blood sugar and energy on an even keel and it helps us avoid temptations. Lastly, don't overlook the importance of hydration. Shoot for a hundred ounces of water daily.*

**Eric Boyette, father of four**

To make things easier, I would also highly suggest you plan out your meals weekly. As in, I would HIGHLY SUGGEST YOU PLAN OUT YOUR MEALS WEEKLY. Take the hint.

Not all guys do this, and I get why. Mick likes to shop the specials and uses the grocery store as a way to get out of the house several times a week. This is a good strategy. Getting out of the house is the best way to keep your mind active. However, I like doing a weekly shop and cutting down the trips to the store as much as possible. For me, this frees up more time for adventures and less time for chores. I find that the happy medium here is to order your groceries online if at all possible. This way, it's easier to plan your meals, control your spending, and shop the specials. With online shopping, I also save about 15 percent of my grocery budget just by not grabbing the "extras" that are never on the shopping list. These are things you typically don't need, like cookies and little coloring books that for some reason cost twenty bucks. Coloring book publishers are making a killing.

> ## DAD HACK
> Grocery store scavenger hunt: For toddlers, print off the pictures of several items on your grocery list. Choose things that they can easily find, such as milk or bread. Now grocery shopping is a game. This keeps them active and engaged and helps prevent meltdowns.

## Because Dad Says So . . .

*The two most important tools in the kitchen are a good knife and a great pan. I am a huge fan of cast iron. A good pan should be thick walled and hold heat, and a great cast-iron pan can do it all. Sear, sauté, fry, and broil. It can go from the stove to the oven. You can even bake breads and pies in one.*

*For knives, there are three that you need in your kitchen. A chef's knife, a serrated knife, and a fillet knife. Remember, knives are tools and you are going to use them a lot, so get ones that you really like. Find the style and weight that fits. If you use steel, you shouldn't have to sharpen them more than once every year or two.*

*Finally, get the kids in the kitchen to help with the cooking. I bought my daughter a steel finger guard to help her learn to cut. I spend most of my day in the kitchen and as a result, so do my kids. Things take longer, it makes a bigger mess, but it also builds wonderful memories and skills! But the biggest benefit I found is that my kids are more likely to try a new thing if they helped make it.*

**Matt Strain, father of two**

## TIPS FOR COOKING 1,092 MEALS WHILE CHILDREN PLOT YOUR DOOM

To be successful when you cook that many meals, you need to be able to do twelve things at once. There you go, that's how you do it. You learn to bend space and time so that you can change a diaper, find the pacifier, and not burn the chicken. It's quite amazing. If you lack magical abilities to change the laws of physics, here are a few things to keep in mind.

1. **The slow cooker.** When you have an infant or a new walker, slow cookers are great for keeping your hands free, and you can add ingredients throughout the whole day. It's a whole genre of cooking that does let you do twelve things at once. This is as magical as it fucking gets.

2. **One-pot meals.** A perfect cooking option for when you have toddlers. Although not as relaxing as the slow cooker or as angry as the pressure cooker, the one-pot meal will save you cleanup and time. Soups, stir-fries, and casseroles are great. There is a reason why your mom cooked so many. If you have a toddler, let them help by adding ingredients to the casserole dish.

3. **The grill.** If you have a child who's walking, your grill is really handy. I love my grill. I use it way more than the stove for cooking. With a grill, there is a lot less cleanup. In the summer, the kids can play outside while I cook. I don't need to watch the grill as closely as I do a pan. I know exactly how long the chicken needs to cook before I turn it. You know how I know this? Because I've been doing this for twelve years, which means I've made 13,104 meals.

4. **The pressure cooker.** When you have kids in activities or when life gets busy, the pressure cooker is your friend. Think of it as a Crockpot that has been working out at

the gym for the past several years. It's an angry cooker,
but that means it works twice as fast. It's still one-pot
cooking, but quicker. On those days that you forget to
take the chicken out of the freezer, a good pressure
cooker will get it done in thirty minutes.

5. **The smoker.** This is dad territory. Smoking is more art
than science. It's based on personal taste and gives the
opportunity to make a ton of dad jokes. I love Jake's
smoked meat. A smoker going all day makes for some
wonderful meals that evening. It allows you to go do
other chores around the house while your dinner cooks.
At the end of the day, get together with some other dads
and just talk about smoked meat for the next three hours.
I have no idea why this happens, but it does. I'm just
saying that men are very proud of their smoked meat.

## The Dad's Cookbook

### MAX'S AUSTRALIAN SMOKED SALMON

*Rub salmon with 50 percent sugar, 50 percent salt mix.
Cover and put it in the fridge overnight, then wash it off
under the tap the next morning. Pat dry with paper towels.
Place salmon on the far side of your grill or smoker. Cook
low and slow, with just a thin slice of white smoke. Chef's
choice for wood, although I like jarrah wood pieces, with
a few wet. Cook from 2 to 3 hours. Serve with a side of
potato salad and fresh sour cream and dill.*

**Max Boronovskis, father of two**

### JEFFERY'S CHICKEN POTPIE RICE CASSEROLE

*Ingredients: 3 to 4 cups cooked rice, 1 pound cooked chicken (cubed), 1 can cream of chicken soup, ¾ cup milk, 1 cup sour cream, 1 cup shredded cheese, 2 cups vegetables (chef's choice), salt and pepper to taste.*

*Mix all ingredients and add to casserole dish. Top with more cheese if desired. Cook at 350°F for 45 to 50 minutes until top is browned. Serve as is or with crispy onions on top. Great way to reuse leftover chicken or rice.*

**Jeffery Bernstein, father of twins**

### SJOBERG'S WORKINGMAN'S HAMBURGER GRAVY WITH MASHED POTATOES

*Ingredients: 1 pound ground beef, ½ yellow onion (diced), 2 garlic cloves (peeled and minced), 2 tablespoons butter, ¼–½ cup flour (as needed), 2 cups water, 1 cup milk, 1 can corn. Homemade or instant mashed potatoes as needed.*

*Brown ground beef and add diced yellow onion. Add minced garlic, simmer. Once browned, do not drain! Add butter and allow to melt. Add flour ¼ cup at a time and stir, allowing it to soak up the juices. Simmer for 1 minute. Slowly add some of the water and stir. Add milk. Simmer. Add more water until the gravy is the consistency you wish. Add corn. Simmer and reduce until it rolls off the spoon. Pour hamburger gravy over mashed potatoes. Prepare to do yard work immediately upon completion of the meal.*

**Erik Sjoberg, father of four**

## BRANDON'S VEGETARIAN TACOS

*Ingredients: 2 tablespoons olive oil, 1 large yellow onion
(diced), 2 tablespoons garlic (minced), 2 large sweet
potatoes (peeled and cubed), 3 tablespoons fresh cilantro
(chopped), 1 cup spinach (optional), taco seasoning to
taste, beans, rice, lime juice, tortillas.*

*Combine olive oil, onion, garlic, and sweet potatoes in
large pan. Cook on medium-high heat until sweet potatoes
are soft. Mash potato mixture into a chunky consistency.
Add cilantro, spinach (if using), and taco seasoning.
Simmer. Serve over warm tortilla and layer with beans
and rice and a fresh squeeze of lime juice.*

**Brandon Cole, father of two**

## HOSSMAN'S FAMILY CHICKEN STIR-FRY

*Ingredients: 2 tablespoons olive oil, 2 chicken breasts
(cubed), ½ red onion (cubed), 2 cloves garlic (diced), ¼
cup water, 1 green bell pepper (chopped), 1 red bell pepper
(chopped), 1 cup broccoli (chopped), 1 cup carrots (sliced),
1 tablespoon grated ginger, pinch of salt and pepper to
taste, 1 bottle premade stir-fry sauce, instant rice or
noodles depending on your taste.*

*In a large skillet, add 1 tablespoon of the olive oil and
heat. When oil is hot, add the chicken and cook
thoroughly. Remove chicken from pan and set aside. In
the same pan, add remaining tablespoon of olive oil and
sauté onion and garlic until translucent. Add ¼ cup water
and all the vegetables. Stir and cover for about 8 minutes*

on medium heat or until vegetables are softened, stirring occasionally. Return chicken to the pan and add ginger, salt, and pepper. Mix. Add your choice of stir-fry sauce (ours is mostly a mix of teriyaki and soy sauce). Heat until the sauce is warm and serve over a bed of rice or noodles.

**Shannon Carpenter, father of three**

## MATT'S COOKING WITH KIDS PUTTANESCA SAUCE

Ingredients: 3 (or more) garlic cloves, 3 tablespoons olive oil, 3 (or more) anchovy fillets (trust me, you'll want these), 28 ounce can whole plum tomatoes, ½ cup pitted black olives, 2 tablespoons capers (drained), red pepper flakes to taste, salt and pepper, fresh Italian herbs.

Begin with teaching the kids to chop the garlic while using their finger guard. (A finger guard is a small shield designed to protect little fingers, and is easily found online.) Warm 2 tablespoons of the olive oil with garlic and anchovies in skillet over medium-low heat. Cook and stir until garlic is lightly golden. Drain tomatoes and crush with a fork or hands (kids love crushing!) in a large bowl. Raise heat to medium-high and cook, stirring occasionally until tomatoes break down and the mixture becomes saucy, about 10 minutes. Stir in olives, capers, and red pepper flakes. Reduce heat to low and simmer. Cook pasta of your choice until tender but not mushy, and drain quickly. Toss the pasta into the sauce and mix. Add salt and pepper to taste. Drizzle with remaining olive oil and garnish with fresh herbs.

**Matt Strain, father of two**

## COOKING STRATEGIES

Yup, just like we did for cleaning, we are getting back to straight-up strategies for cooking. In fact, many are the same. Declutter, prep early, do one load of laundry while you cook. All solid advice that can be applied to cooking for a family. However, with cooking, it really comes down to how you manage the chaos that surrounds you. Not every day is going to be a one-pot meal or Crockpot night. Some days, you need to kick it up a notch and have multiple pans going while constantly stirring the béarnaise sauce. Doing this with children around is the challenge. While I've cooked on one leg while fending off charging toddlers with the other, I do not recommend it. Once the toddlers organize, it's over. There are things you can do so that you have the time to cook a wonderful meal safely.

1. **Baby jails.** The baby carrier is not a good idea while cooking. Those little feet like to kick stove tops. What does work well are baby gates, Exersaucers, and high chairs. Keep them near but not too near, enough that you can still interact with the little ones and throw Cheerios at them. When you have an infant around, these are your absolute best bet.

2. **Kid help.** Same as with cleaning, let them pour stuff into other stuff. Let them mix the marinade. Pull out ingredients from the fridge. And then TEACH as you go. See, look at that, taking an ordinary everyday moment and making it a teaching experience. This becomes a habit pretty quick, and as soon as you get it, we send you your dad sweater in the mail.

> **DAD HACK**
>
> If you have a smart-home device, like an Amazon Echo or Google Home, let the kids set the timers and the music. The device can also read your recipes and help with ingredient substitutions.

3. **Distractions.** There are special toys that I pulled out only when I needed my hands free to cook. When the meal was done, the toys went back up. Whether that is a doll or a bunch of crayons, find what works for you. Although don't be surprised if a crayon ends up in the mac and cheese. You can also use screen time and get into an endless debate about how much time the kids spend on electronics. There are pros and cons here. For example, a toddler may accidentally order thirty-two decorative pillows while searching for a YouTube video. Then it turns into a whole argument because they don't match the bedspread and you've got a thing with your partner now. However, it does keep toddlers busy when you've got multiple pots going. I've watched the entire *Scooby-Doo* catalog while making smothered pork chops. Make up your mind and do what works for you. You'll get no judgment in this book. Shit needs to get done.

4. **Backup meals.** Not everything you are going to cook is going to be edible. And although I can give you an A for effort, the crowd still gets cranky when they don't get fed. Keep some frozen meals in the fridge that can be easily nuked or baked. I always have a frozen pizza handy. When it's gone, I make sure I put it on the shopping list

for next time. Just have something on hand for when that mustard sauce comes out looking like a science experiment.

5. **Premade meals.** This is one of those things that you discover and think, *Wow, I didn't realize there was an entire fucking cult organized around this.* However, sometimes cultists get it right. Look up recipes for premade meals. Spend a whole day cooking and box it all away to be heated up for later. It requires more work on the front end but on busy weekday nights, it really helps. Here's a tip: Don't cook and freeze scrambled eggs. They don't reheat well and taste like rubber.

## Dad's Premade Pesto

*The fresher the ingredients, the better the pesto! Stays good in the fridge for up to three days. Large bunch of basil (3 cups), 3 garlic cloves peeled, dash of salt, pepper to taste, ½ cup extra-virgin olive oil, ¼ cup feta cheese, 1 tablespoon cream cheese, splash of milk. Mix in a food processor until creamy. Mix into premade pasta or rice, or use as a dip.*

**Sol Jorge Moscol, father of two**

6. **Steak for you!** You read that right. A lot of our significant others have to travel for work from time to time. We at-home parents take this time to stop cooking complicated meals and just nugget up. And while that's fine, there's a better way. Let the kids eat the hot dogs, nuggets, or whatever. Take the time to make a good meal for you.

When the spouse is gone for a long time and you get no breaks, this is your reward. It hit me one day when my wife started actually complaining about having to go to another client dinner. "I'm getting so tired of steak," she said. I almost divorced her right there. Then I realized that if she was eating steak, then so was I. Spend the money, get yourself a steak. A potato is a dollar. Enjoy. You've earned it.

## DINNERTIME: THE PICKY EATER AND COMING TOGETHER

It's a brutal truth that kids don't care about the effort it takes to make dinner. As such, there are a lot of meals they just won't eat. If it's not nugget shaped, then it might as well be asphalt. The picky eater is very vocal, and if they could write, they would give you very bad online reviews. To this day, no one in my family will eat my pan-seared chicken with mustard sauce. It's a damn work of art, and yet they all turn their noses up at it.

For the picky eater, allow them the food rule of three. The child gets three foods that they never have to eat. Simple, right? There is a catch, though, because life is full of catches. They can't change those three foods out for three months. Once something is off the list, it can't go back on. What you are doing here is giving the picky eater a choice and some control. It also saves the argument for later. My kids tried to game the system and change per meal until I promptly got up and made whatever they just took off the list. Dad is a clever bastard.

Finally, I want to add a word about actually sitting down to eat dinner as a family, regardless of what age the kids are. This is the glue that will hold your family together when things get tough. It also gives everyone a chance to talk about their day. Ask your kids open-ended questions. Don't go for yes and no answers. Then do the same with your partner.

> ### DAD HACK
> Our family's three dinner questions.
>   1. What was the best part of your day?
>   2. What was the hardest part of your day?
>   3. What did you do that was kind today?

It may look like dinner is relaxed and spontaneous, but it's a carefully conducted symphony designed to share the load of parenting. Give each person a chance to talk about their day and actually listen. And I mean really LISTEN. What matters in their lives must matter in yours. I know life is busy, and I know things get crazy with kid activities and with responsibilities. I sometimes have weeks where I don't get home until nine every night. But as soon as I can, I make sure we have a sit-down dinner.

Remember that the sit-down dinner is just as important for you and your significant other as it is for your children. Engage them; talk about their day and yours. Plan tomorrow's day. Take an interest in what is bothering your spouse. It pays off in the long run. You're not the only one who has made sacrifices to stay home with the kids. They have given up some of that bonding time, and there may be guilt. You may not have noticed yet, but there is a whole working-mom versus at-home mom battle raging out there. It's stupid, but it is what it is. Alleviate some of her fears and worries by giving her this time.

If you have a baby that has to be fed by hand, still sit together at the table as a family. Eat in shifts with the rule that no one is done until everyone is done. This was my respite during the early years. It was a chance for my wife and me to get on the same page and just decompress. I know way more about project management and corporate time sheets than I ever should.

What really breaks you during the grind is a feeling that you are fighting everything at once by yourself. It's so consuming that it's easy to get wrapped up in your own head with your endless responsibilities. Talking about them in a positive setting is the best way to make it through.

## FROM THE DADS GROUP

**MICK:** Take a look at canning. You have control over all the ingredients, which means you control the amount of preservatives. Most have a shelf life of at least a year. If you do it properly, it will last and give the kids a good healthy snack. Salsa, jelly, or applesauce. They are simple. You can pickle anything, like carrots! They also make great gifts.*

**LARRY:** A few deck pots with seasonal herbs are easy to grow and it's nice to always have fresh basil on hand. Also, get to know your Crockpots! I have several to use depending on what I'm cooking. Some run hotter than others, so experiment and know their

---

* Author's note: At this point, I had to cut Mick off because my God he can talk about canning for a really long time. I was afraid he was about to bring out a slideshow of his favorite jars. In his defense, though, he cans fantastic salsa.

temperatures. My bigger one cooks hotter, thus faster. It's not good for keeping things warm.

**JAKE:** For my smoker, I use the FireBoard thermometer. It is cloud based so I get notifications on my phone as the meat smokes. I also use a Thermapen digital thermometer to double-check that the meat is done.

**MIKE:** If you cook a lot with charcoal like a true purist, unlike Shannon and his gas, now is the time to invest in a chimney starter. You can typically find them for under twenty bucks, and they make grilling over charcoal easy.

## Because Dad Says So . . .

*Need to keep your energy up but the kids are napping? Coffee grinder in the garage does the trick without waking them.*

**Patrick Wilbraham, father of three**

# YOU STILL HAVE TO DO DAD CHORES. SORRY ABOUT THAT BUT AT LEAST YOU CAN DRINK A BEER ON A WEDNESDAY AFTERNOON WHILE YOU MOW.

We at-home dads find ourselves in a very unique position. I don't know how to break it to you, but you are still expected to do all the working dad things as well as cleaning, cooking, and handling the insane asylum. Well, probably expected. You know what, now that I think about it, I think we do this to ourselves. I cannot remember actually having this conversation with my wife. Fuck it, I'm going home right now to tell my wife that she needs to mow the yard today and patch the hole in the wall that the kids put there when they were playing golf inside the house. I feel like this is a big moment for us stay-at home dads! The revolution has begun! Wish me luck, fellas!

It didn't go well.

So, apparently, we are required to do all the honey-do chores that working dads do. My argument that at-home moms don't have to replace water heaters did not go well. I was promptly shown videos and articles of all the repairs a lot of at-home moms do around the house. I said, "Great! Then you can mow the yard, too!" That made things worse.

## HOME REPAIRS

It is a well-known fact that kids fucking break everything. If any of us were smart, we would hire them out as demolition crews. I would set up a playdate at your site, and in an hour everything would be rubble. We would still get nap time in, which I would demand we do on the clock because my kids are union.

When fixing things around the house, nothing goes according to plan. For example, I built window screens. I did this because all of our stupid windows are custom built for some stupid reason, and brand-new stupid screens are more expensive than the stupid windows. After three days of work, I had wonderful new screens. However, when I turned my back, Vivi decided that they needed purple glitter glue. She was helping. Does it bother me that my window screens look like unicorns had an LSD rave? No, it does not. I love them because my daughter did it and all the artwork she does is wonderful. Let's get to some tips to help home repairs go a bit smoother.

## ≡ All the Shit My Kids Have Broken

*Mick's basement. Mick's giant potted plants. Kitchen table snapped in half. A historic Mormon jail. Window screens. The hood of my car. Two cell phones in toilet. Game controller in dishwasher. Dishwasher. Garage door motor. Mike's hammock. Hot tub cover at a rental house. Walls: holes, markers, and general mayhem. Nine iron. Spreader. Wheelbarrow. Automatic car door motor. Lawn mower. Leaf blower. Nine-person tent. Nebraska. This list is now too long. I'm going to stop before my insurance agent sees the rest.*

**Tip 1:** Things are not going to go according to plan. Accept it so you can keep your frustration down.

*At the very least, I have a wonderful story to tell the HOA about why I have purple window screens. They've been on there for nine years. It's faded but Vivi promises she will give it another coat as soon as she's done fucking up my car with a hammer.*

*I worked three days on those window screens. In my head, the job should have taken less than a day. This is when I was a newish at-home dad and I was stupid, just like my windows. This brings me to tip number two.*

***Tip 2:*** However long you think the chore should take, multiply that time by a factor of three.

*Every home repair chore you are going to do will take longer than you think. It's because you are working in a world of constant distractions. Chaos is your new normal and, in the chaos, someone gets the glue out and goes apeshit. Then you spend another whole day figuring out how to get glue off things until you just say, "Fuck it," and roll with the punches.*

## DAD HACK

To remove glue from walls, get a bucket of hot water and soak a sponge. Gently scrub the glue and let the heat do the work. Repeat as necessary.

*Here's an honest truth without any jokes attached so you know how much I really mean it. There is no one in this world that I would rather have help me with home repairs than my kids. I'm dead serious. Give me my daughter and two sons and I'm a happy camper. They are awesome.*

*My kids are eager to learn. They want to know what I'm doing and why I am doing it. They want to know how things like screens are built. They want to know what the tools are called. They retain that knowledge so very, very well. So sure, it can go a little slower, but it's also a big help.*

*Once, I was installing a microwave above the oven and dropped my screwdriver. My boy Ollie, just three at the time, came over and then picked it up and gave it to me, which was great because I was holding the microwave up with one arm and microwaves are very heavy. I took the time to tell him what kind of screwdriver it was (Phillips), and now he will go get me one when I need it. He knows where it is stored.*

**Tip 3:** Take the time to teach your kids what you are doing and why you are doing it. Show them the ins and outs, and as time passes, you'll want them helping you more than anyone else.

*My wife is good at many things, like writing marketing plans and leading meetings. She is a terrible house-repair helper. Totally sucks at it. She never calls things by the right name, and lord forbid if I ask her to get me a socket wrench with a three-quarter-inch socket. I always get a set of pliers. "This thingy? Does it fit on that thingy?" Just give me my daughter. Vivi can replace a car battery.*

*As for dealing with the frustration, there is an uncouth way to help you deal with that, but it does have a pretty great side effect. Your children will pick up all kinds of new and great cusswords. And then they can repeat them IN PROPER CONTEXT. I wouldn't recommend this in public, or making other people aware of it, but c'mon, it's a bit funny when a four-year-old tells the cat to "fucking move" when you are taking the dryer apart.*

**Tip 4:** Don't teach your kids to cuss, but when they do, give them credit if it's said in the right context.

**Tip 5:** YouTube and the internet are your friends. And you can always mine your local library for the total and complete knowledge of home repair.

*Someone, somewhere, has had to replace a dryer belt from a GE machine built in 2001. It's that specific. And that someone, an angel among us mortals, has made a video of it and put it online.*

*I do need to add a caveat to the last of this. I am very, very lucky to have a set of wonderful friends and fathers in my life. Together, we have redone kitchens and bathrooms. Jake helped with the piping on a new water heater on a Sunday morning. Another dad from my group, John, came over and taught me how to replace the blower motor on my furnace. Mick has a chainsaw. Larry can replace broken glass in doors. Mike can fix a motor on an automatic sliding van door. It's these friendships that have carried me through the last twelve years, and I wouldn't have been able to write this book without them. And when you point out how helpful they have been, they will give you a "meh" like it's no big deal. They don't want any special recognition for what their friendship has meant. But fuck it, I'm going to give it anyway and then hug each and every one of them. Mostly because they will be extremely uncomfortable with such a public display of man love, and I find that very funny. It's going to be even funnier when I get all mushy in the book, and I will make sure I*

*read this part at a public reading to get as much embar-*
*rassment out of it as I can. But seriously, thank you.*

**Tip 6:** Hug your guys. It's okay to show a little vulnerability
and appreciation from time to time. Don't worry if you
don't have guys yet. We are going to cover that.

## MOWING THE LAWN

This is the one chore we can never escape, and there are a couple
of ways to deal with it. For the purpose of this section, I'm not
going to discuss proper lawn mower technique or how you should
make your stripes in your lawn. Each man has his own standards
and policies, and I respect that.

It's the actual act of mowing that is difficult, though, especially when the kids are younger. You can't have them around the
mower, as it is a machine of death. Here are some strategies that
will help you get the mowing done. Each father of my dads group
does it his own way.

**Mick's Mow:** When Mick's kids were younger, he would do it
during nap time and keep the baby monitor on his hip.
This is actually a very good tactic, as he knew that he
had a good two hours most afternoons. It also made
him look like a cyborg. Just make sure your baby monitor has a good range and check it often to make sure you
can hear anything as you go about your mow. This
would work well for Mick because his yard is very large
with a lot of trees. He needed two hours just to get the
front done.

**Shannon's Popsicle Sprint Mow:** This was my preferred method. The kids would sit on the porch and eat Popsicles. They knew they were not allowed off the porch. My job was to finish mowing the front or back yard (each a different day) before they could finish their treats.

My yard is pretty small, and if I hustled, I could get the front yard done just in time. It also counts as a great workout. For the backyard, we have a deck, so the kids were more contained and liked throwing shit at my head when I passed underneath them.

**Jake's Early Morning Mow:** Jake is one of those people who likes to get up at six and shower. I'm guessing he does this with mowing as well, although I'm not sure, as I'm still sleeping. I imagine his neighbors hate him for it.

**Mike's Weekend Mow:** Mike just does it on the weekend while his wife watches the kids. He says that he has mowed plenty of times with the kids around during the week, but he's lying, and we can't trust anything he says. But it is a viable strategy that is probably the safest.

**Larry's Nubbin Touch-Up Mow:** Larry lives on the biggest property of the dads. As a result of the many hours spent maintaining his grass, he has grown overconfident. Thus, one day Larry thought he would get in a quick touch-up mow the day before all of us and our families came over for our annual family picnic. Larry wore flip-flops. Normally, Larry is a very deliberate and smart man. Normally.

In a series of unfortunate but completely fucking foreseeable events, Larry was mowing underneath his playground while wearing those flip-flops. Larry pulled the mower back, tripped, and mowed over his toes.

To set everyone at ease, Larry is fine although a little lighter in the toe department. He didn't cut off all his toes, just the tops of a couple of them. As a result, Larry saves a ton of money on pedicures. Larry put his bandaged foot in a turkey pan so he wouldn't bleed all over the car's carpets, and his wife drove him to the hospital. Larry received care and also made a new product: toenail garden mulch.

As his good friends, once we made sure he was okay, we have continued to make fun of him for years because of this incident. It's how men bond. It's weird. We all acknowledge that.

Which nickname do you guys like better, (1) Larry of the Eight Toes, (2) Nubbin Lover, or (3) Toe-Knuckle? I'm going with number three and shall immortalize this story for the whole world forever. Larry Toe-Knuckle.

Also, in typical Larry fashion, he still attended the family picnic, because hell if he isn't tough. Good on you, Toe-Knuckle. Good on you.

## FROM THE DADS GROUP

**MICK:** Sometimes things just need to get done. That means, if you have to, give kids some screen time to distract them so you can make a repair. Don't beat yourself up. It's okay for the kids to chill out.

**LARRY:** Don't mow with flip-flops on.

**JAKE:** Do all the prep work with the kids. It makes them feel like they are contributing without breaking anything. Then when it's time to get the more serious things done, they typically get bored and can entertain themselves for a bit. If they can't, then stop your chore and interact with them and get back to it when you can. Kids also make a great pair of extra hands to go grab a screw or a socket wrench, so take advantage of that while you can.

**MIKE:** Save the bigger projects for the weekend when you have help from your spouse. There are some things that you can't have your kids around, especially when they are babies. With babies, you basically have nap time and weekends for chores. So, don't expect to get a lot done when they are around. It's okay to let those chores wait if something is going to be dangerous or complicated.

# HOW TO TAKE ADVANTAGE OF MAGNIFICENT DISASTERS

It's those moments when the whole world goes to shit that you find not only your strength but also the motivation to make it through one more day. They make your decision to stay home with the kids worthwhile. The hard part is to recognize them and to act on those moments. How do you separate them from the daily monotony or write them off as just one more thing to do? Do not confuse these moments with chores or a to-do list. This is your payday, and Daddy needs a new memory.

What am I talking about? What are those moments? They are more than the first steps or words. The moments I'm talking about are the unusual disasters that occur when you get to teach a life lesson or help your children make sense of the world. Those failures of planning, circumstance, or overconfidence  hat make everything worth it. You connect with your kid on a deeper level than you thought possible. I'm talking about the moments that are so specific to your family that they become part of your legend. And sometimes they are so small, so insignificant, that it's hard to tell what they are.

Here's my example. Early one morning, the cat brought a dead baby bunny to our back porch. Except, when I discovered that bunny, it wasn't dead. But the poor thing was close, and my heart broke because baby bunnies are about the cutest things ever. I did what Dad has to do. I didn't have a choice. I cannot watch something suffer. It's not in me, and the bunny was too far gone to help any other way. I went and got my shovel and brought it to the back porch. I lifted the shovel and chopped the head off that baby bunny. I hated every minute of it. As soon as the sharpened blade made the thunk on the wood, I heard my four-year-old daughter gasp. I turned around and saw her three-year-old brother, Wyatt, eating dry toast right next to her.

Shit fuck. I forgot about the kids. I got wrapped up in the day-to-day of parenting. This was another chore, another repair, another problem to take care of. And what did my kids, who used to think of me as a hero, think of their father as he committed bunny murder? All that hard work, two years of staying home with them, down the drain. I'm a bunny murderer now, which in their world is about the worst thing you can be.

"Daddy," Vivi said. "What happened?" She ran over to me as

I still held the shovel of failed fatherhood. Her little brother and his dry toast came with her, as a proper toady should. I stood there. I didn't know what to say. I didn't know what I could do to make them unsee the thing that they clearly did see. This is the first thing they are going to talk about in therapy in their early thirties. Their bloodthirsty father who killed baby bunnies.

"Honey," I said. There was no out. I told her the truth. Not the whole truth, as we'll see, but enough so she could make sense of it. "The bunny was hurt really bad and wasn't going to live. We can't stand by and watch it suffer."

"Why was it hurt, Daddy?" she asked. When she calls me Daddy, my insides melt. I considered becoming Dr. Frankenstein to take this back. Surely I could cyborg this shit to make it work. What's the going rate on souls to the devil? Is there a genie shop around here? When my little girl or boy looks up to me with those expectant eyes, all big and innocent, I break. Can't help it. Just happens. The only thing keeping me from buying her a pony is a single income, although if I sold enough blood over the next couple of years, I could probably make that happen.

"Well, baby," I said, finally trying to answer her question. "Some animals hunt. And they bring them to our porch . . ."

"Was it a hawk, Daddy?" my daughter asked.

And here's my lie. In a moment of panic, I made an executive decision. My children love the cat. My children can also be vindictive little buttholes. I've already lost the bunny. I didn't want to lose the cat. Not that they would have gone that far, but I am saying that my daughter punched the nurse when she saw Mommy hurting with contractions when her brother was born. She ran out of my arms at four a.m. and started waling on that nurse enough so that I asked if I could leave a tip for the excellent services rendered at the hospital. I didn't want that to happen to the cat. So yes, we blamed a hawk that they had seen on TV the day before.

"Yup. It was a hawk. Terrible really, but it's what hawks do. Hawks gotta eat. Bunnies are hawk Lunchables. Goes well with some wild rice." I went with the lie.

Immediately, my daughter ran back inside. A moment later, she came back with our dog, a boxer that is 100 percent muscle and has a really loud bark. He is a complete wimp, of course, but my daughter didn't know that. He looked and sounded fantastic.

"C'mon, Khan!" she said. "Let's go get that hawk!" See, I was right to be concerned about the cat. And yes, I named my dog after *The Wrath of Khan*. I love him. I couldn't have made it through this without that dog.

Here was that teachable moment, though. We got dressed and put that poor bunny in a shoebox. We had a funeral, where my daughter wore a white dress and my son finished up his other piece of toast. My daughter even had a little umbrella in the mid-morning sun. It was the saddest and cutest thing I have ever seen. And later, we went hawk hunting.

I took the time, though, to begin the very hard conversation about life and death. What happens after and where do we go? What happens when we die? That is an extraordinarily hard conversation to have with one so young. But when she really needs to understand it, maybe it won't be such a shock. We spent the whole day doing this. Nothing was cleaned. No dinners were cooked. We had frozen pizza ready for Mom when she got home to a dirty house. My wife understood.

These are the moments that I'm talking about. Now, don't go chopping heads off bunnies, but learn to recognize those teachable moments. These are the reasons that we stay home. We want to be the ones to teach our kids these lessons because they are hard to know and hard to understand. It can be very abstract to talk about, much less to teach. But in these moments and in your kids' memories, this is the most Dad you will ever be.

Sometimes you have to manufacture these moments. You take an adventure to a museum and talk about some of the harder parts of history. It's for a purpose. You are here to teach. Make it happen. It doesn't have to be such a sad subject either. No reason to go all Kafka on them. A kindness to a stranger, or an appreciative word to a server, and then an explanation to the kids of why you acted the way you did. Your kids will 100 percent treat people the way they have seen you treat people. Which makes me scared for the bunnies of the world. But it is a truth. Your model of manhood is the one that will stick with them the longest. Don't fuck it up. This is the weight that is now on your shoulders and pushes down on you in the middle of the night. We all feel this, and if you're a new dad, this is one of the first things you discover.

Approach these times with intention and thought. Sure, you're winging it because we all are, but it doesn't mean we don't think about it all the fucking time. You don't have to be Superman to have your kids think you are.

For the record, years later I told my kids the truth about what happened. When they could really understand death and what that means, as well as the nature of animals, I told them it was the cat. My daughter was ten, my son was eight, and the cat was very old and safe. This story is now in my memory savings account. This is what makes it all worth it.

# CHAPTER 3

# YOUR DADS GROUP

Why and how to find your social support.
Don't go it alone; take one of these with you.

---

### WORDS OF WISDOM

Being thrust into a new and unfamiliar phase of my life was a bit frightening. I was most surprised that there weren't more opportunities for fathers to connect. They just didn't exist. I wanted to talk about parenting, sports, and the changes happening in our lives. I joined a dads group to explore and to be with a like-minded crew of dads.

*Lance Somerfield, father of two,*
*cofounder of City Dads Group*

---

I hit one of my lowest points of being an at-home dad at the four-month mark. Erin and I had moved to Kansas City. We lived in a really tiny rental house. The dining area was so close to the living room that the kitchen table touched our aging green sofa. Our bed couldn't fit in the master bedroom, so for three months we had to sleep on a mattress on the floor. Vivi and

Wyatt, ages two years and six months, shared a room. This is where I hit my bottom.

Isolation messes with my head. It's subtle, too, because when it gets really bad, I can't even see that it is getting worse. I turn inward and everything I do seems to be not good enough. I know that we are all our own worst critics, but it got dark for me.

When Erin came home from work, I would pounce on her, and not in the good sexy-times way. I would literally wait by the door until she opened it. From the second she said, "Hi! How was your day!" I would spew word vomit all over her. Not about anything interesting, but just eager to talk to someone. Anyone.

"Hey, I cleaned the kitchen and then I cleaned the bathroom and after that I cleaned the kitchen again because we made lunch which was peanut butter and jelly sandwiches then the kids took a nap . . ."

Somewhere in there, I hope I at least took a breath. If you ask Erin, she will probably say that I didn't.

It felt good to talk. I didn't even care what I was talking about. There was no beginning or end to my word salad, just a smorgasbord of gibberish. If you think it's boring to clean, imagine listening to someone telling you they cleaned like they're giving you the box score of a Junior League Golf match.

For months I did this to Erin, and she sat there and listened. Every day. For months. Marriage is about communication and being there for your partner. But do you really want to hear about how your partner used circular strokes to clean the toilet instead of up-and-down strokes? No. It sucks. Ask Erin.

One day she said something that hurt. "Honey, you need to find friends."

That stung. I had fucking tried! Do you really want to know

what it was like to be a stay-at-home dad twelve years ago? Let me fucking tell you.

Right before Wyatt was born, a mom was chatting Erin up at the grocery store while I checked out. The lady handed my wife a card when she noticed my wife was pregnant. "Why don't you join our moms group," she said to Erin.

"Oh, my husband is going to be staying home," my wife said.

I swear to God if there was a fainting couch next to her, that mom would have gone down clutching her pearls. She actually snatched her card BACK and said, "Good luck," as she and her bouncy ponytail pranced away. Erin and I looked at each other as if trying to believe we had seen what we had clearly just seen.

That was just the beginning. In the months since the move, I had sent enough emails to moms groups to completely clog all the email traffic on the internet. Know what I got back? Half the time it was "Thanks but no thanks" or no response at all. Fucking nothing.

That's the kind of isolation I'm talking about here.

I would go to story time at the local library and sit by myself. I could manspread all I wanted to. Half the time, people didn't even want to make eye contact. And when things like that start to happen, you turn on yourself. You start seeing things that aren't there. You become self-conscious. Do I smell? Do I have a booger?

When I tried to start conversations, there would only be a polite smile at best. Maybe I would also get a head nod as the other parent scooped their child up and moved away from me. I spent the majority of those first four months convinced that I was creepy and scary. I did my absolute best to look like Mister Rogers. Still, not one single meaningful conversation happened. Not one.

In this book, I talk about the value of your self-worth because I fucking know what it's like to not have it. To not know that what we do makes a difference. I fucking know. In those early months, I felt like a complete failure. I didn't think that I was contributing to the family at all. Isolation has a knack for taking the worst things we think about ourselves and magnifying them so much that they're all we can see. It escalates from there. I became a bit paranoid and sometimes felt that what I was doing was illegal. That really happened. Fleeting thoughts, sure, but they came up. A police car drove by my home early one day, and I honestly had a moment when I believed they were there for me. How can a man care for children? Shouldn't he get a job? Not only did I feel worthless, I felt like a criminal.

My wife says that I have a hero complex. I like to be "the guy." I have to come in and fix the problems, give support, or offer a shoulder. And she's right, I do enjoy all of that. But what happens when you don't see yourself as the guy you want to be? You spiral, and the isolation is there to make it worse. If I strip away all the jokes and images of "Heroic Shannon," what's left makes me cringe. I want to help that guy. I want to pull him aside and tell him to have confidence in himself. I want to tell him that he will find his way.

I got out of the house as much as possible during those months. Play places, story times, and even the mall playground. The fucking mall playground. What happened at the mall playground?

A month before Erin told me that I needed to find friends, I sat next to a bench at the mall playground while Vivi played and Wyatt slept in my lap. I was reading a book and had my arm across a tiny part of the seat. A moms group came over to the bench and put their bags on the ground, and then one of them sat on my arm. I don't mean next to it. I mean actually on it.

I panicked. Early me was trying my hardest not to intimidate people or come off as creepy. I was trying to be approachable. Instead, I got sat on. I didn't move. She didn't move. It appeared that not only did she not see me, she didn't register that I existed. And there I was, getting sat on at the mall playground.

It couldn't have been more than ten seconds, but it felt like forever. I had a slight panic attack as I tried to play this scenario out in my head. *I'm touching this lady's ass. She's going to freak. I'm going to end up in mall jail and have to explain to my daughter why Daddy is on the sex offender's list.*

I'm sure my cheeks flushed. This is where the isolation and what it does really comes into play in our own heads. Even though I had not moved a muscle, I was embarrassed for myself. The longer she sat on me, the more the embarrassment grew to humiliation. Not only did I not matter in the parenting world, I didn't matter at all. I was invisible. I didn't exist. That's what it was like to be an at-home dad in the early days. Invisible. A failure. Alone.

I eventually said, "Excuse me," and the mom gave me a nasty look. She is also the model for the "Whatever Mom" joke in the first chapter. That lady is real. I've met her several times.

"Honey, you need to get some friends," my wife said. *Yeah, no shit. I'm trying.*

My wife and I talked about my getting friends that night as we lay on our mattress on the floor.

"I'm not going to make it," I told her. "I need help." Now I felt like a bigger fuckup. Who am I to complain? I have a kick-ass wife and family. I'm a guy who gets to stay home with the kids all day and raise them. I didn't believe that my feelings were valid, and thought that if I could suck it up, things would be fine. Over and over in my head, I convinced myself that the isolation didn't matter. I could hack it. I could be tough. I was miserable.

A week later my wife came home and said she found something on the internet that I might want to have a look at. The landing page read KC Dads and explained that they were a dads group and open to new members. At the bottom of the page was an email address.

Yup, my wife found the dads group that I would eventually join. At the time, I didn't even realize that was a thing, and I had no idea how much it would change me. It shifted my foundation so much that I can't imagine my life now without Mick, Jake, Larry, or Mike, and a hundred other guys.

I'm going to tell you how I met Mick, the leader of KC Dads, and I'm going to do it in the form of a romance novel because it's the only way I feel comfortable expressing this kind of emotion.

I first met Mick at the zoo. I had made contact through the email Erin found, and he actually wrote me back. My heart fluttered.

Mick had a daughter Wyatt's age, a son Vivi's age, and creamy brown eyes that a man looking for friends can get lost in. Sitting at a picnic table at the zoo, Mick said that he had been an at-home dad for two years. He enjoyed going on outings and feeding Cheerios to his daughter. He wanted to be my friend, and I loved him at first sight. *Do you love me, Mick? Mick, do you love me? Love me, Mick!*

Mick told me the rules of the dads group, the manly code that manly men live by while trying to care for their children. His sultry voice, sometimes high pitched when he gets excited, told me that he, too, was looking for friendship in a forbidden world.

"Playgroup switches between members' houses each week. They are on Wednesday and start at ten a.m. Guys stay no later than two but many leave a bit early because of nap time schedules," Mick said. *And your shoulders are very masculine,* I'm sure he thought but held back. Somewhere in the zoo, a silverback gorilla roared.

"It's important to keep to a schedule with the kids," Mick said. His thick black hair bristled in the light breeze as he continued his speech. "We do a dads night out as well. Just a couple of us head to a bar to watch a game or just hang out without the kids." His words washed over me like motor oil on a hot steamy engine.

"So that's it. That's the dads group. Our membership goes up and down. We usually get five to six guys coming to playgroups. Sometimes more, sometimes less, depending on what's going on. Any questions?"

That's how I joined my dads group. With them, I found my self-worth. I found the value that I add to my family. I found my Mick.

Things are different when you go out with a dads group. Jake likes to call us magical unicorns. There is something fantastic about seeing ten guys pushing strollers through the state fair. Guys who know what they are doing and aren't apologetic about doing it well. We have been stopped and asked to pose for pictures. No shit, actual pictures. More than once.

As a group, we are an attraction rather than the oddity. With my dads group, I learned to stop giving a shit about whether people were okay with what I did for a living. What the hell does that matter to me? I found my confidence.

This is what I'm trying to give you in this book. You've seen dads in the sidebars and the callout sections. This is your dads group now, so hopefully you never have to go through what I did. Or if you're there now, this is your way out. Mick is still here. He can give the welcome speech in a throaty, sultry voice.

Things have changed a lot over the last twelve years. At-home dads are more numerous now than ever. And moms are way, way more accepting. Many have welcomed the stay-at-home dad into their groups. I do my best in this book not to give moms any shit because people are just people and I don't like tearing others down. Plus, I also know how much crap moms have to put up with that I never have to. But in the beginning, ladies, some of you were absolute shit heels. You're cool now, but it's been an interesting transformation to witness. Although, if I'm honest, I still have a lot of space at the library story times. The difference now, though, is that I don't care.

I found my tribe.

Dads, I can help you find yours.

## HOW TO FIND YOUR DADS GROUP

Let's cut through all the drama and mystery right from the start. The best way to find a dads group of your own is to go to City Dads Group. The first thing you need to really know about dads groups is that we don't do drama and we're organized. Dads groups are practical. There is no mystery with us, it is what it is. Dads groups make for very boring movie-of-the-week material but are great for men who need to find a parenting support group.

City Dads Group grew out of the dads group in New York. They did it well enough that eventually other guys around the country would email asking how they did it. Thus, City Dads Group was born. Part of their mission is to offer support and advocacy for those navigating fatherhood. And they've done a damn fine job. They mentor dads groups all over the country and have an up-to-date, easily searchable list right on their website. Currently, there are forty City Dads chapters all across the country. They are located in many major metropolitan areas of the US, and there is one in Toronto, Canada. Go, maple syrup. (I don't know much about Canada.)

Portland, Minneapolis, Chicago, DC, Dallas, Austin, Omaha, Kansas City, Sacramento—there are City Dads Groups everywhere. There's even one in Anchorage, Alaska. You want to talk about whether stay-at-home dads are manly or not? These dudes change diapers and deal with bears. So, the next time someone gives you shit, ask if they could handle a playgroup while keeping an eye out for bears. That's manly as fuck.

City Dads Group should be the first result on your Google search when you type in the name. They also have a podcast, a new-dad boot camp, articles about fatherhood written by fathers, and a ton of other stuff. This is one of the resources that I would have loved when I first started out. I would have had someone to talk to about getting sat on.

## Because Dad Says So . . .

*Be a part of the change that you want to see in the very beginning. Dads are equal parents and need support just like any other parent. Find your group, or if not, start your own. Be persistent and patient and make this one of the resources that every dad deserves. Also, bears aren't a big deal. Shannon is overplaying it.**

**Mike Jenks, father of one, Anchorage City Dads Group**

---

\* Author's note: Only Anchorage dads can downplay parenting with fucking bears.

# WHERE TO LOOK WHEN THERE IS NO ESTABLISHED DADS GROUP

What do you do if you don't live in one of the City Dads Group areas? What if you're in a small town or not near a metropolitan area? Do you hang out with cows and wheat?

First off, cows and wheat are awesome, and if that is where you feel at home, then you do you. I get it, there's a lot of land out there, and I'm not going to forget about anyone. Our dads in Middle America, of which I am one, have a different set of problems. No dad is left behind in this book because like I said, I know what it's like to be alone. So screw that, let's help everyone.

You need a group, and we are going to help you find one. Begin by engaging your community. Believe me, there are other dads out there. What I mean by engaging your community is to start talking to people who run the places where parents go.

The library should be your first stop. Get to know your children's librarian. She is going to be your new best friend. If there is a dads group around, then she will be the one to know. Her whole day is spent around parenting groups. My children's librarian is named Claire and she is about as close to a superhero as I have ever found. She actually recruited for my dads group. We left her a stack of cards, and every time a dad would come in, she was quick to hand that card out. Go find your Claire. You'll know it's her because she smells like rainbows, and when she smiles, children become well-behaved readers.

You also need to hit up the community centers in your area. Every town has something, a place where there are gyms or where parents come together. Community centers also usually do a great job of advertising on their boards. One of the dads up in Minnesota used to place fliers all over his community, including these centers. Dads are out there looking for you as much as you are looking for them. I've had guys come online and state that there are no dads groups in their area, only for a bunch of us to point them in the right direction.

Also keep in mind all the other places that parents congregate. Play gyms, grocery stores—you'll find your dads at all of these. New dads love these joints because they are safe and easy. They feel comfortable here and that's where you want to meet them. You'll identify the dad by the head nod we give each other. It's like a secret handshake. Plenty of dads have met at the park first and translated that into a meetup later.

If any of that doesn't work, we're not done yet. We haven't even gotten to the technology. Check out the apps Meetup and Nextdoor. Many dads groups advertise themselves on these apps and are actively seeking new members. Make sure you broaden your horizons. Driving through the county to get someplace is a daily occurrence for many of my small-town dads, so a meetup thirty miles away isn't something that is beyond the realm of possibility.

My point is go to where parents usually go and make some friends. This is really difficult for my introverted dads, and I get that. I've known enough of them to see the challenges that they face. Be brave and go say hi to another dad. Strike up a conversation after you've seen him around story hour.

Let's say you can't find a dads group. Yes, a moms group can be an excellent option. If you can't find any dads after trying everything you can, then give them a shot. I was actually part of a moms group for a very short time before my wife and I moved.

My old work partner, Tricia, brought me to hers. Once Tricia vouched for me, I was accepted, and it was amazing. That moms group showed me what to pack in my adventure bag and how to do a one-handed diaper change. I owe them a lot for that first month when Erin was gone. Without them, I doubt I would have made it. So, moms who were there, consider this a very heartfelt thank-you for inviting me to your outings.

Parenting groups are also an excellent option. You can find these through churches, community centers, or neighborhood message boards. They are a great place to meet other dads. Even if no other dads come, you can be the first. There is nothing wrong with being the first. I have found parenting groups to be much more welcoming to the at-home dad.

Even after all that, you may be coming up short. It happens. But believe me when I tell you we are everywhere. There is another dad out there feeling the exact same thing you are—that isolation. He needs a hero.

That's you. This is your chance to be the hero. You need to start your own dads group. We are all here cheering you on and ready to show you how to do it. Neil Armstrong didn't stutter-step, and neither should you.

## FROM THE DADS GROUP

**MICK:** Local parenting magazines are an excellent way to find your dads group. We advertised in ours for years and would find guys that way.

**LARRY:** Look to the people that you constantly run into all the time. At-home dad or not, it doesn't matter. Don't get hung up on titles and worry about who is the primary caregiver. Just find your friendships.

**JAKE:** Start talking about water heaters, and the dads will come running. Or notice the guys who are at the hardware stores with their children. This is great dad territory.

**MIKE:** Start simple. Sometimes there is nothing else to do but to keep putting yourself out there. Take heart in that and keep going. Keep trying to meet other dads.

# BE THE HERO AND START YOUR OWN DADS GROUP

When you can't find a dads group, it's time for you to start one. Yes, it takes a bit of work and dedication, but by now you should see what the benefits are. It's a place where you can ask questions without judgment. For example, when Erin was breastfeeding, her nipples cracked. This freaked me out because I had no idea this was a thing. They actually bled. Erin cried. Vivi cried. I stood there without a clue in the world.

## *Because Dad Says So . . .*

*When you start a dads group, you need to be the guy or get a team of guys who want to build a community. Be assertive and think outside the box. Always hustle to get*

*your name and your group out there. You're not trying to*
*satisfy loneliness; you are trying to build something bigger*
*than yourself. A good dads group fuels you and brings*
*energy to your life.*

**Matt Schneider, father of two, NYC Dads Group**
**and cofounder of City Dads Group**

This isn't the Disney version of parenting that I had been sold. Who the hell knew about cracked nipples? I didn't know what to do to help, and it's really impossible to see my wife and daughter crying without me wanting to help. But what was I supposed to do? Who could I ask that wouldn't be condescending or think I was some sort of weirdo? Was I supposed to ask my own doctor during my prostate exam? "Hey, while you're rooting around back there, let's talk about cracked nipples."

My next thought was to ask our pediatrician. Was I going to just bring up the topic all nonchalant right after she asked if the baby was pooping? It's not that I couldn't, but it was more that I didn't feel comfortable asking that question, and a million others like them.

When you look online, so much of what you see in parenting-world advice is geared toward moms. They play off dad as a secondary character in his own story. That's not me. That's not us. I need answers that aren't condescending.

And to answer your question, yes nipples can crack during breastfeeding. There are ointments and nipple shields that you can buy that help. Would have been nice to know that before it happened, though.

This is why you need a dads group. If you can't find a dads group, start one.

First, follow Larry's advice from earlier: Don't try to limit yourself to "full-time stay-at-home dads." Open it up to every dad. It doesn't matter if they are the primary caregiver or not. It's all just terms that we use to classify things because for some reason that makes all of us feel better.

There are dads out there that work irregular schedules—firefighters, police officers, night shift workers, retail workers—and many of them have taken on the primary care duties of their children. Even if there are no other at-home dads around you, I guarantee you there are dads out there who want to have someplace where they feel supported. Dads like this have all run through my own group.

That's part one of creating your new dads group. Here's what else you can do.

### 1. Establish an internet presence.

This is how most of the guys will find you. Name your dads group to be very specific to your area. If you're in a small town, open it up to the entire county. There are plenty of web services out there that will host a web page for free, or skip the web page completely and host it on Meetup or on a Discord server, as long as it's easy to find and states specifically what you are and how to get in contact with you.

### 2. Get with the social media.

I know, many of us hate the use of social media, but it is still a valuable tool. Facebook seems to be the most popular but don't discount Instagram or Twitter. Keep it up-to-date so that guys looking for you can see that you are still active. When you do an adventure or a playgroup, put something out there.

> ## DAD HACK
>
> Have playgroups at members' houses. This gives guys with babies or who are nervous a safe place to go where they will be able to exert a little bit of control. It's fine to have playgroups at parks and play places, but always have at least one a month in the home.

**3. Set the rules and times.**

Rules let other dads know exactly what to expect. Start with how often you plan to meet up. Pick any day that works for you. After all, you are in charge, and if it doesn't work for you, who's going to run this thing? In a bit I'll give you our schedule as a guideline. Also, set a time that recurs every week. This lets other dads know that if they missed the first playgroup, there are more to come.

**4. New members have to come to one playgroup before they get a schedule.**

This rule worked well for us. Basically, when a new member wishes to join, they have to come to one playgroup first. They learn where it's going to be by making the initial contact. Mick follows up twice with guys who don't make it to the first one, but after that, they are on their own to contact him again. This also ensures that you are not giving anyone access to addresses or contact info without meeting the person first. I hate scam artists, and at-home parents are a prime target for them.

## 5. No selling at dads group.

This is our hard-and-fast rule. We've had guys try to join just to network or to sell us insurance or run a multilevel marketing scam. That's gonna be a hard no from us. A dads group is a place for the kids to make friends and for the dads to find support. It's not about building your résumé. I wouldn't even pimp this book at a playgroup. That's how seriously we take this rule.

## 6. As you grow, delegate responsibility.

This will keep other guys invested over the long term as they now have a say in how the group works. For example, Mick handled our overall leadership and promotion. Jake did the dads night out schedule. Larry was on web development. We tried to play to everyone's strengths. My job was to set the adventures and to make new guys feel welcome. My role works better for an extroverted individual. They still call me Julie the Cruise Director. It was supposed to be an insult, but screw those guys, I'm awesome at finding adventures. Call me Julie all you want, I'm over here finding the World's Largest Pair of Underwear. What you are looking for is a leadership team.

### Because Dad Says So . . .

*Carry fliers around in your car. Every time you make a stop during your day, ask if you can leave one. My fliers had little tear-outs that had our website or other contact information. I left them at grocery stores, community centers, and even gas stations. Leave them everywhere parents go, not just the expected places.*

**Chris Brandenburg, father of one, Twin Cities Dads Group**

## 7. Advertise everywhere.

Find your inner marketer and get to work. Paper your town as much as you can. Talk to people who own or run the places that you go. Be prepared with a short speech to tell people exactly what your group does and how you do it. Have business cards printed up with your website and social media contacts and hand them out freely.

## 8. If it's not working, change it.

This is the true beauty of a dads group. We do what works, not what other people expect of us. If your weekly schedule isn't working for all the guys or for you, change it up until it does. Tweak it as things go on.

**STARTING A DADS** group does not have to be complicated, but it does take dedication and hard work. You've got to want to do this. To use a saying from my own father, you have to go whole hog. I met my guys in 2008 at a point where I was not doing well. When I'm isolated, things get bad in my head. My group helped me work through that isolation. At one point, our smallest membership at a playgroup was two. However, Mick took us to the next level, and I like to think that I had something to do with that. But let's give credit where credit is due. Mick knows his shit. He'll be all humble about it, but when it comes to leading a dads group, my little Iowan farmer gets the job done.

Our biggest playgroup was forty-one people. It was huge and I felt a little bit bad for our host, Jake. He's introverted by nature and does not enjoy large crowds. However, I enjoyed watching him cringe all day as he was trying to keep up with the hot dogs. Over the years, hundreds of dads have run through our group in one way or another. We've gone from small, to large, to small again. It all depends on the guys you have with you. And I'm happy to say, twelve years later, I'm still with that core group of guys even though all of our kids are now in school. We still meet for a breakfast weekly and see movies all the time. It has become more than a dads group. They have become part of my family. Mick is the emergency contact on all my children's forms.

## FROM THE DADS GROUP

**MICK:** You'd be surprised how many places know the dads who are the primary caregivers. All the local moms know. Talk to people and hand out that card.

**LARRY:** Trial and error is good. We changed things around a lot until we found something that worked for us. Not only playgroup days, but also Friday adventures and Rebel Tuesdays. We were routinely seeing each other four to five times a week when the kids were little.

**JAKE:** Be consistent with your schedule. Make sure it's out there and that people are coming. The more

> consistent you are, the more buy-in you'll get from
> other guys.
>
> **MIKE:** Don't forget about the wives! Encourage them
> to have their own moms night out. If they mesh, it
> makes it easier on you.

# NOW THAT YOU HAVE A DADS GROUP, HOW DO YOU RUN IT?

I get the question a lot: What do you guys actually do in a dads group? If I'm completely honest here, the question bothers me a bit because it assumes that as a father, I have no idea what to do with a group of kids. That somehow the act of parenting is unnatural or weird. That's a little messed up. I usually tell people that we rob banks but not to worry because all the kids are in five-point-restraint car seats.

What do dads do when we get together in a group? We parent, talk about sports, change diapers, deal with meltdowns, work on cars, whatever. I do what I would normally do but add kid activities to it. Just because I'm the primary caregiver does not mean that I forgot how to be a guy. And it certainly doesn't mean that I don't know how to comfort and nurture my child.

Now, a bigger question for you new at-home dads: How do you run a dads group? I'll give you our schedule and our best practices. Just keep in mind that this is a guide only; feel free to take the ideas that work for you and your group and ditch the ones that don't. And if you get asked, "What do you do in a dads group?" just rip these pages out of the book and hand it to them.

> ### Brian's Five Guidelines to Run and Grow a Successful Dads Group
>
> 1. *Care about people and share that passion.*
> 2. *Make it a point to have a personal connection with each member.*
> 3. *Offer to co-host an event with a new member to build engagement.*
> 4. *Plan out at least two months ahead and be consistent.*
> 5. *Build your leadership team from members and delegate.*
>
> **Brian Dykes, father of two, Chicago Dads Group**

1. **Playgroup.** Held every Wednesday from ten a.m. until two p.m. When the kids were younger, everyone took off by one to keep up nap schedules. We rotated who hosted based on a schedule that Mick or Jake came up with. Not everyone in the group hosted and it wasn't required. However, the more guys you have that are willing to host the easier it is on everyone. I would host a playgroup at my house once every two or three months. The kids were free to play, or we were all on the floor. As they grew, they needed us less and less, so the dads sat around the table talking, playing board games, or asking for advice on whatever was on our minds. What we don't do is gossip. It never came up with us. For the longest time, I had no idea what the wives did for a living. Dads are usually not the gossiping type. In the summer, when

things got too big for anyone's house, as older kids would
be out of school, we switched to a park. Mike is a damn
good park grill master. The host supplied lunch, which
was usually an assortment of fruit, chips, and hot dogs.

2. **Dads night out.** Once a month, we would leave all
parenting responsibilities at home. Sometimes it was a bar
or a pool hall. Other times we would see a movie or go
bowling. It didn't matter. It was a chance for us to have a
break and build our friendships. It was a place where we
could unwind. Different guys would plan it as the need
arose. I WOULD HIGHLY RECOMEND THAT YOU
DO THIS.

3. **Friday adventures.** I wanted more than just once-a-week
meetups. I wanted to explore. There is no museum,
history thing, or field that I haven't seen in the Kansas
City area. Some days, one or two dads would come.
Other times, the whole group would attend. I rarely
missed a Friday adventure. We even had a standing
appointment at the downtown library with Claire. She
has watched our kids grow up and is as much a part of
the group as I am. She helped teach my kids to read.

4. **Rebel Tuesdays.** Sometimes I may have gone overboard.
Okay, I went overboard a lot. Rebel Tuesdays were our
generic term for when someone wanted to do an
adventure that wasn't planned for Friday and didn't
interfere with playgroup. It was a lot looser in the
planning and nothing was scheduled. Some days eight
dads would come, and on others, none would show and I
would go by myself with the kids. The chocolate tour
came to my town when Vivi and Wyatt were still under

four. I invited everyone, but no one came. That was fine because hell yeah I'm going on a chocolate tour no matter who tags along. The tour was a bunch of videos on chocolate making and a couple of beans under glass cases. But the whole place smelled like chocolate, almost as if there were fresh brownies waiting for us at the end. There were not. They just piped in the scent for the exhibit. Anyway, I turned the kids loose on them. Don't worry, those people can't hurt us anymore.

5. **Twice-yearly family events.** It was important to us that our dads group wasn't just about the dads and kids. We were smart enough to know that this was something that the whole family was participating in. Every year we held a summer picnic for everyone, as well as a Christmas party. The picnic eventually turned into a drive-in movie night that is still our tradition. The Christmas party occurred because as at-home dads, we never get invited to parties anymore.

6. **Moms night out.** You know what, this wasn't even our doing. It wasn't Mick or me who suggested the wives get together. They did that all on their own. They didn't even tell us. One night, Erin just said she was going out with the other moms. After seeing how happy she was when she came home that night, I knew that it was something that I wanted to encourage. Our wives have their own unique challenges as the sole breadwinners of the family. They need a place where they can bond with other women who do the same thing. They have sacrificed as much as we have for our families. Their Moms Night Out was their support and something they continue to do

many years later. Their friendships are as strong as ours. Erin, Amy, Amanda, Jane, and Kelly talk way more than we do. They tend to get deep, while we make a lot of dick jokes. Encourage your wives to do this; it's one of the ways you can protect your marriage.

7. **Yearly dads trip.** Every year, my dads group and I hit the open road and do a yearly dads trip. We have just completed year ten. Just the dads and the kids, no moms. The moms get together while we are gone and have a whole week of quiet. They eat out a lot. Our goal is to see the strangest, weirdest stuff that we can find in a state that we haven't been to yet. You haven't lived until you've seen seven minivans cruising down the highway somewhere in rural Nebraska. This trip creates the memories that I live on. It's taking the time you have with the kids and making the most of it. Not every day is going to be magical, but some are. We have been to Nebraska, Kansas, Iowa (twice because Mick has a hard-on for Iowa), Missouri, Minnesota, and Oklahoma. By the time you read this, we will be hitting Kentucky.

**DO WHAT WORKS** for your dads group. I've said it enough but it's important, so I'm saying again. These are all just examples of how you can run your group. We've all been that one guy at the park before. We've all gotten the looks, and sometimes someone wants to confront you. I know enough guys who have had the police called, as insane as that sounds. Alone, we are looked at with suspicion. But together? Together we are something magical. It's not just my group either.

The New York dads seem to be in the newspapers every week. Even here in the middle of America, I've done my fair share of television interviews. *Redbook* magazine once called us the Adventure Dads. When I've got all my dads together, I'm not alone anymore, and someone is watching out for me. For that, I can't tell you how much I owe them. Go get yourself a dads group. It's an adventure worth having.

## FROM THE DADS GROUP

**MICK:** Invite people into your home and spend real time with them. The more time you have friends over, the closer your bonds will become. That's going to pay off down the road. And it also gives them a safe place where it is okay to come and to know that any disaster can be handled. Playgroup was almost like a break for us.

**LARRY:** Give new members a chance to pick the next activity. This causes engagement and buy-in with new members. If they feel more invested, they'll participate more. On your next Friday adventure, ask where the new guy would like to go that he hasn't been to yet.

**JAKE:** Find your people. Take away all of Shannon's pretty words and that's what it comes down to. Find your people, even you introverted guys. Put down the phones and start building those relationships. Give them a chance to ask questions that they don't feel they can ask anywhere else. This is one of the greatest things about a dads group.

**MIKE:** Group communication is one of the most important things to remember with a new group. Make sure you're putting out emails every week. Reminders, ideas, welcoming new members. This is a big deal. Communicate with each other. It gets everyone on the same page and lets the new guys know that they are welcomed. Include them in that as much as possible.

# AND IF YOU CAN'T FIND OR START A DADS GROUP?

We're not done yet. Like I said, in this book we are helping everyone. All dads, you guys deserve this. My rural dads, my metro dads, my dads who don't like big in-person groups. The dads who are introverted or who can't drive. All my dads who work part-time or full-time jobs and still want to find support. I've got you.

This thing is bigger than any of you realize.

Welcome to the National At-Home Dad Network. I told you, dads are organized as fuck.

The National At-Home Dad Network focuses on the four pillars of advocacy, community, education, and support. That's a fancy way of saying they are the national organization of at-home dads who are there when you need them, and not just in person. When you want to find your online community, these are the guys you want.

## ≡ Because Dad Says So . . .

*It is easy to create a barrier and not reveal your full self.
You need to find guys that you can connect with in a
conversation. You'll find yourself relieving some of those
burdens that you carry. That's where a sense of
community comes from. It allows each of us to break
down our barriers. Where we don't feel manly enough, or
smart enough, or good enough. You are not alone. You're
not the only one dealing with these issues.*

**Jonathan Heisey-Grove, father of two, president of
the National At-Home Dad Network**

They not only run several online groups, but their whole
premise is that no dad has to walk this path alone. They are guys
who can help you through it all. Want to know who these guys
are? Take a look in this book. The Dad Hacks, the "Because Dad
Says So . . ." boxes, the chapter opening quotes—many of the
dads quoted are members of the National At-Home Dad Network. The organization has been around for years and they understand what you are going through.

They excel at connecting fathers and supporting anyone,
members or not, who needs it. This is what they do. This is their
job. When you need a good place to go online and get real-life-
tested strategies, this is where you go. Just search their name on
Google, Facebook, or whatever media you prefer. They have a
presence. It doesn't even have to be about parenting, because we
are more than that.

Dads who brew beer, dads who write, dads who build kick-ass

pillow forts—they are all there. In ten minutes, you can get the right oven temperature to bake bread and the correct ignition timing of a 1984 Dodge. I'm not even remotely kidding. They are from every walk of life, and they are there to help. Some come from different countries. You don't realize it, but some of the dads you are getting advice from aren't in America. In fact, an Aussie gave one of his recipes in an earlier chapter.

These are your people. This is your support. And it gets better.

We have a national convention. It rotates to different parts of the country every year so that guys who couldn't go one year can go the next. There are scholarships as well. You'll learn everything you need to during the convention. Think of it as professional development. From learning to communicate more effectively with your child's teacher to learning about nutrition for babies, it's at the convention.

It's where I learned to do my daughter's hair. I took a hairstyling class. The stylist, a father, taught forty of us how to do French braids. We had little mannequins in front of us, brushes, and something called detangler spray. Look, I'm bald. I knew nothing about hair. And to my Vivi, Daddy is so sorry for the early years.

When I took a crack at my mannequin, by the time I was done, the poor thing looked like it had the mange. For the record, Mick can do a really good braid. This is where he learned it.

Everything that we read online and in magazines is geared toward moms and has a tendency to treat dads like total dipshits. "Oh, look at Dad! We better make sure he knows that diapers go on the butt!" Get that condescending shit out of here. That's the Homer Simpson dad who is afraid to try, doesn't want to be around his kids, and sometimes might cook a dinner. That cliché needs to go away, and so do the articles that detail those efforts.

Sure, I mess up a lot but I always learn. Those failures are what have made me a better father. And the community of dads is here to give you better advice and more on-point information without being a dick about it. When you have a question, ask the guys online and they'll help you out.

There're more conferences, as well.

Dad 2.0 focuses on changing the face of fatherhood. It abhors the Homer Simpson dad. The goal is to connect fathers and improve the conversation around parenting. If you are a writer, YouTuber, or other content creator, this is the conference you want to attend. It celebrates dads who are taking an active role in their children's lives and helping them put that content out there. It's a huge conference that gives us dads a place to connect and network. Hell, a big part of this book came about because of the encouragement and connections that I made there. I am forever in their debt. Sponsors like Huggies and Dove Men have shown up in force. And also, NFL Hall of Famer Ronnie Lott put his hand on my shoulder at this conference. I haven't washed it since. I don't care how I smell, it was Ronnie Lott!

Do me a favor, ditch all those bullshit parenting sites that talk to dads like they're fucking idiots. There's plenty of other places that celebrate fatherhood. Fatherly, Life of Dad, and the Good Men Project to name just a few. This is where you'll find your tribe, and we are always accepting new members.

City Dads Group, the National At-Home Dad Network, Dad 2.0—I told you we are organized.

## FROM THE DADS GROUP

**MICK:** Layer your ponytails. Start with a high tail with a third of the hair blended into the middle, then another hair tie. Then finish up at the bottom with one hair tie holding all three smaller ponytails together. It's a cheap workingman's version of a French braid. If you put your ponytail at four o'clock versus six o'clock, it rides better in the car seat.

**LARRY:** When you are at the convention, make sure you charge all your drinks to your good friend Shannon so that he will one day write a book and ask you constantly for advice. That way, it all evens out.*

**JAKE:** Look to make connections within your hobbies. You'll find a lot of dads in there that are doing the best they can just like you. Getting involved in those communities is a great place to connect. Don't limit yourself just to "dad things." Expand yourself.

**MIKE:** . . .

**ME:** Tell me what you would tell new guys about reading those parenting websites that are geared toward moms.

**MIKE:** Don't read them, how about that?

**ME:** That's solid advice.

---

* Author's note: Yes, this happened. They all freaking owe me for the very high-end beer they ended up drinking on my tab. On a fun note, drunk Jake likes to hug a lot. Who knew? The man has a soft spot in there.

# CHAPTER 4

# YOUR MENTAL HEALTH, THE MOMS, AND OTHER RELATIONSHIPS

It's okay when things get weird, but knowing what to do in that moment is what really matters.

## WORDS OF WISDOM

We are a group of fixers, and that makes it really hard when dealing with your mental health. It doesn't feel natural when we can't correct something. And when we can't fix stuff, we strike out. Recognize that in yourself and then have the courage to get the tools you need to act differently. The tools are there, but it requires you to be honest with yourself. You can't hide your mental health issues. You can't sugarcoat it. That's the hard part. Lots of bad shit is going to happen and you can't fight all the battles on your own. You can't always fix it. You are a work in progress. Believe me, I've lived it.

*David Stanley, father of one*

'm afraid that when you read this you will see me how I see myself sometimes. A guy who doesn't have all the answers and is weak. There is the word I was looking for.

When I talk about my own mental health, I feel weak.

And why should I care what you think of me? Haven't I been making that point over and over again in this book? But when it comes to my own mental health, that word, *weak,* pops into my head every single damn time. When I talk to myself about this, I mostly refuse to use the words *depression* and *anxiety* because of that feeling of being a weak man.

I worry that if I give them their official names, I will somehow make them real. Not only that, but that I don't deserve to feel them. That I am a pretender and not worthy of feeling anything at all. I am afraid that I am co-opting the experiences of other dads who have gone before me, and I'm trying to profit off their pain.

So I label my depression and anxiety by euphemisms. Words and phrases like *my low time* or *nervousness.* Those are my code words, and admitting it here makes me want to delete all these words. I don't want you to read them, because it's a piece of myself that I've tried very hard to cover up. That's why I tell so many dick jokes. That, and a good dick joke is funny.

But the jokes have always been a way to protect myself. This is what I do when it comes to my mental health. I throw up shields and make up words that don't matter. All so I don't have to admit that I have mental health issues.

What happens when I quit hiding behind the dick jokes? You and I have to be honest, and that's going to be hard. Screw it, let's be honest.

A year into being an at-home dad, in the middle of winter, during a cold stretch where the clouds covered the sun for days, I felt something was off. I was lethargic. I was unmotivated. I began to think of myself as a failure.

I was robotic with the kids. It's hard to explain to you now, but I was on this relentless schedule where I was doing the same thing every day. I should have been happy—another deflection that has no business repeating itself in my head. And it wasn't that I wasn't happy, it's just that I wasn't . . . present. Bedtime could never come fast enough.

Erin could tell something was wrong and cornered me several times.

"What's wrong?" she asked.

"Just tired," I said, which is the short answer I give when I don't want to talk about what is going on.

Eventually, whatever "funk" I was in (another euphemism) went away. I read books about seasonal depression and convinced myself that I didn't have it because that is what weak men have. Erin tried several times to get me help. I brushed her off again and again.

Another winter came. I was off.

And there it is, the first time that I've said this out loud to anyone that wasn't my wife or my therapist. Now you know, and I feel exposed. You know what? It's not a fun place to be, and I desperately want to tell another dick joke here just to take the eyes off me. But we've already come this far together so let's keep going. Let's talk about the "other" thing I don't want to discuss. Also, fuck, this is hard.

My anxiety didn't start until years later, not really. Or it was probably always there, but previously I called it by a different name. Anxiety is harder for me than depression, something that I am still reluctant to accept because I feel like I'm lying. I wish I were braver, like the dads I have seen who can talk about their mental health without having to whisper it.

Some days I don't know where my anxiety comes from. Everything is going well. I shouldn't feel the tightening in the chest or the needles going down my forearms. My fists clench and unclench constantly. The kids are happy, my wife is happy, and everything is Disney perfect. But it doesn't feel fine. On those days, the hardest that I have, I lose my patience easily. At first, I tried to think my way out of it. I would try to convince myself that I didn't deserve to be anxious. When that didn't work, I gave myself a pep talk: grow up, take it like a man, tough this out. Those don't work either.

My wife's hand on my arm works. I'm not sure why. But it does.

On other days, I know exactly where the anxiety comes from. It comes from when I am feeling emotionally overwhelmed and that there is too much in my life. Almost like there is too much to feel? Does that even make sense? It's like an avalanche that comes crashing down on me, and I can't manage those emotions very well. When I try, because I'm supposed to be tough, I can't control it. Everything spirals and my thinking gets cloudy. Just getting me to make a decision, any decision, is too much to ask.

As at-home dads, we feel that so many things are our responsibility. Every dad in this book will be nodding their heads to that statement. We all get it, and you probably do as well. Every problem in everyone's life comes to our doorstep. "Dad! Dad! Dad!" they scream. You make it through one disaster only to be met with another. Fix it, Dad. Dad can fix it.

Chest tightens. Needles in the forearms. Fists clenched.

Those are the really tough days, and my best strategy is to go to my dads. They understand and know exactly what I want to say when I absolutely don't have the words to say it. It's just being around them that helps. They are primarily how I have protected myself from depression and anxiety. Or not *protected*. That's not the right word here either. They saved me during some very bad times, and I don't think they have any idea. Well, come with me and I'll tell you how they did it. I'll share this, one of my worst moments, and they'll see how they helped. Now you will be able to see me when I was so overwhelmed that I couldn't really function. And you'll know what I mean when I say having a support system in place is essential.

Let me give you the setup so you can jump right into the story. Within a span of days, I got the call that Penguin wanted to publish this book, my brother-in-law died, my van started blowing smoke in the middle-of-nowhere Iowa, and then I killed a bunch of butterflies. That's the story we are going to get into; enjoy the ride.

As I mentioned earlier, every year the dads and I take the kids on a road trip. It's an annual event that we all look forward to. And with the book contract recently being signed, I was eager to be around them more and just celebrate. Unfortunately, my brother-in-law passed away the day before we were to leave. He was one of my best friends, and I've known him since I was sixteen. I was the guy who married his best friend's sister. I know, I broke the guy code but it's worth it. My wife is awesome.

But when he died so soon after my good news, I had these two competing emotions in me. They were battling for attention, and I couldn't give that to either of them. One is enough; both at the same time felt impossible. I was overwhelmed. I decided that I needed to go on the dads trip because I needed to be with my guys. The funeral was a week away, and my wife had flown down to Texas to begin making arrangements. That left me with the kids and all of this to navigate. And I knew the kids needed help with their loss as well. They needed their friends around them to help them cope. He was their uncle and a great one at that. So we went on the dads trip through rural Iowa and parts of Minnesota.

One moment, I was on the phone with my agent, who was handling so much. There were so many details to go over. He doesn't realize how much that meant to me either. He's a dad, too, by the way. And then in the very next moment, I would get a call from Erin and her family about the funeral. I would give advice or take on one of the many tasks that something like that involves.

Sometimes on the road I was laughing with the kids and singing along to loud music. But when they were in other cars, with their friends, I cried. Then I would laugh. Then I would cry. A victory and a tragedy all within four days. Even now, I'm thinking, *Holy shit, that was a lot to process.*

Then we killed a thousand butterflies. How's that for a kick in the teeth?

Apparently, in late summer in the countryside of Iowa, butterflies migrate. And on a road that I will never remember, we ran right through the middle of them. Motherfucker.

"What's that?" my youngest son Ollie asked as they splattered on my windshield leaving gross weird green smears that looked like I felt.

"Um . . ." I didn't want to talk about death anymore.

When we stopped, we found the dead butterflies stuck to the grilles of our vans. The very absurdity of this week was almost too much for me to take. And now, the butterflies. Mick's youngest daughter, Cait, gave me a homemade card with a heart on it saying that she was sorry I was sad. I walked away from the group and cried again. I hid myself from my friends and my children as I was afraid what they would think of me as I broke down.

On the next leg of the trip, my van started to spit white smoke from the tailpipe. That was my breaking point.

I had handled the isolation for so many years. I had made it through seasons of depression. I had been stoic as fuck as I tried to control my anxiety (didn't work). But I couldn't be strong anymore, and those words popped into my head. *I am weak.*

The dads and I pulled over our convoy at a gas station. Jake and Larry popped the hood while Mick and Mike took my kids. I was low on oil. Jake and Larry have more experience with cars than I do, and they just took over while I sat in my van and stared blankly ahead. Eventually, I had to step out and talk to them. They guessed an oil leak and we decided that if we kept checking, we could keep going. Which was good, because I had no fucking clue what to do. We were in the middle of nowhere Iowa, almost to the Minnesota border, I think, but I could be wrong. No town larger than a thousand people anywhere near us. And my van was dying.

Chest tightening. Needles in forearms. Fists clenched.

I got the kids back in and tried to start the car. The van didn't make a sound as I turned the key. And that, my friends, was my wall. That's when I cracked and lost it.

I yelled and screamed. I laughed like a complete nutjob. The panic attack was there in full form, but at least it had a reason this time. Sometimes they happen to me for no reason at all, which makes me feel even weaker. But here in the middle of nowhere fucking Iowa, I was overwhelmed in a perfect storm of emotion that I couldn't control.

Because that is my real trigger. Control. When I don't feel like I have it, no matter what's going on, that's what sets me off. And apparently this goes back to my own father, who had MS since I was five. A lack of control because there are things in my life that I can't do anything about, like seeing my own father succumb to a disease that I wouldn't wish on anyone. And there was never anything I could do about it, no matter how much I tried. I felt helpless constantly. No matter how big I got. No matter how strong. There was nothing I could do.

But I could always make him laugh. Humor. My shield. But right now, at the gas station with everything crashing around me, I felt utterly helpless, just like I had as a kid.

That day at the gas station, with Larry under my hood and me losing my shit, it was Jake who saw me for what I really was, but that's only because the others hadn't told me that they already knew I had previously dealt with mental health stuff. But even before the trip, they fucking knew about my fights with depression and anxiety in the past and were obviously ready to take the burden off with so much going on now. They knew. Buttholes.

"What the hell am I going to do?" I asked Jake. "What the ever-loving fuck am I going to do? My brother-in-law is gone, but I got a book deal! We killed a bunch of goddamn butterflies and my car won't start. What am I going to do? Where the fuck are we, anyway? All I see is freaking soybeans!"

It was not my proudest moment, and I don't want to share it. But there it is. Shannon in full-on panic attack meltdown.

Chest tightening. Needles in forearms. Fists clenched.

And then Jake, big rough-and-tumble Jake, hugged me. How's that for a twist that no one saw coming? You have to understand Jake really well to see what he did for me. Jake is not a hugger. He is not a people person. Jake once stabbed me with a fork for taking one of his french fries. That shit hurt. But here he did what I needed most even though I didn't know what that was. That big lug gave me a hug.

"We are going to get you back on the road. And if the van breaks down, we'll call AAA and get it towed somewhere and pick it up on the way back. We'll pack all your stuff into one of the other vans and continue the trip. We've already decided," Jake said.

Those magnificent sons of bitches made a plan without me because they fucking knew I couldn't handle any more decisions and were just waiting for the right time to take over my burden. So they took all the weight off me. They fixed the van while I talked to Jake. Apparently, the van wouldn't start because a battery terminal had come off when we checked the oil. They tightened it, and for the first time on that trip, I started noticing what was around me.

I'm not fucking around when I say get your dads and build your community.

The rest of the trip was fine. I was escorted for another eight hundred miles. Always two minivans in front and two behind for the entire trip, clearing out butterflies and leaking puffs of smoke out the back. And because you are going to want to know, the van was puffing because it was leaking oil, and apparently I have engine sludge, which I would much rather have than anxiety. We completed the trip, and then I took my family to the funeral. I'm not saying I wasn't overwhelmed then as well, but I am saying that my dads were there when I really needed them. It's something that I will be forever grateful for. That was one of my worst moments as a parent, and I know I'm lucky to have them.

For me, mental health is extremely hard to talk about, which I think is common with a lot of us. When we are young boys, none of our heroes say they are dealing with it or show any weakness. But what I know now, after seeing so many dads share their experiences, is that it's not a weakness. It's bravery, and I'm doing my very best to be like those other dads right now. To give you my experiences so that you can see yourself. I'm not qualified to diagnose anyone, but I can say that I've been there, and I hope you find your connection in these stories.

You and I are jumping into mental health in this chapter. I will try to use as many jokes as I can so we can have our humor shield, but we have to get to it, frankly. You and I have to take away some of that stigma surrounding men's mental health, and then we are going to go through some strategies you can use to protect yourself.

We are also going to talk about the relationships that are around you. Those are your bedrock and they need to be looked after. You don't parent in a vacuum, even though sometimes our minds make us believe we do. Those relationships are your support system—or sometimes the reason your mental health gets worse.

None of this is easy. The isolation can be so hard, and we are at so much risk. It's not talked about in our world, even by those of us who are trying to find the courage to do so. It's because it makes us feel small and inferior. I feel it right now as I consider hitting "delete" on every word I've written. There are a million eyes glaring at me, at these words, and I am exposed. *Vulnerable*— a word that feels as unnatural as *weakness.*

But it is honest. Everything here is as truthful as I can make it. I hope some of you can see yourselves. Stand tall knowing that you are not alone.

First, know that it's okay to get professional help. There is no shame in it, no matter what our stupid man brains tell us. Reach out to your dads and to your community. Whether you are introverted or extroverted, find at least one other person who can see you for who you really are. Then protect the relationships that you will rely on during your absolute worst moments. Get yourself to a therapist who can give you a safe place to talk about all of it and find a way through it. It will be one of the best decisions you've ever made.

## Because Dad Says So . . .

*One morning I woke up and knew that if something didn't change, I'd be looking down a hole I couldn't crawl out of if I didn't take action. If you think there is a problem, then there is one and you need help. Talk to your partner, talk to your friends, and you'll be surprised at how many people are in the same boat. As men, we do what is necessary. Taking care of ourselves is the most masculine thing you can do because last time I checked, it doesn't matter what other people think.*

**Dan Huffman, father of two**

## STRATEGIES FOR PROTECTING
## YOUR MENTAL HEALTH

There are a lot of studies out there that deal with depression and anxiety, and even a few that mention dads and parenting. Not many, though, and sometimes I'm convinced that Dad's mental health is an afterthought when it comes to parenting.

> *Rick:* Hey, I'm bored. We should do a study about dads and depression and anxiety in parenting.
>
> *Bill:* Wait, that's a thing?
>
> *Rick:* I think so. Probably. I don't know, we usually ignore this type of thing.
>
> *Bill:* What does Steve think?
>
> *Rick:* I don't know, he's at home on paternity leave.
>
> *Bill:* Wait, we get paternity leave? That's awesome!
>
> *Rick:* No, we don't. He's just using all his sick leave so he can spend time with his new kid.
>
> *Bill:* Oh, well, that kinda sucks. What's he going to do when his kid is actually sick and he's out of leave?
>
> *Rick:* Kids don't get sick when they are around Dad. I think we've done studies.
>
> *Bill:* Cool. How long does he get off so he can bond with his child? That seems like it should be pretty important.
>
> *Rick:* Three days.
>
> *Bill:* . . .

I'm pretty sure that's how these things get started. But if you read deeper into some of the real studies, you can find some of the risk factors that at-home dads deal with. Once you know what to look for, you can begin to get to the strategies that combat them.

From the American Academy of Pediatrics (they didn't hire Bill and Rick), here are some risk factors with comments by me, because some of these are so obvious that it pisses me off that they were ever ignored in the first place.

**Difficulty developing an attachment with the baby and feeling excluded and jealous over mother-child bonding.** Um, yeah. Well, no shit this is a risk factor. I mean, holy crap, how is attachment to your child not more encouraged for fathers? Fucking hell. See, this is why I have anger issues. How many times have you heard "Oh, I'll take the baby" or "Just give him to me." That needs to stop. The time you spend with your child is crucial for both you and them. Yes, there are going to be problems, but you are going to figure it out because you are a badass who needs to bond with your kid.

**Lack of a good male role model.** This just makes me sad.

**Lack of social support.** One of the literal themes of this book, because this is some massive bullshit.

**Changes in marital relationship.** This is actually a tough one. You have to protect your marriage. We're going to spend some time on this one later.

**Lack of rewards in parenting.** Okay, so this one hits home for me. The focus of so much of the parenting discussion is on moms. But you are not a secondary character in your child's life. This is one we can do something about.

**Maternal depression.** This gets overlooked when it comes to dads. Dads are 100 percent affected by postpartum depression, and to pretend we are not is ludicrous. When my wife hurts, I hurt, and with that hurt comes the feeling of being powerless. Guys who have been through this will tell you that it's not easy on Dad. I'm not going to minimize what moms go through, but I am making the case that it's important for dads to recognize our own limitations and feelings as well.

**Financial and work stress.** This one makes my anxiety go off the charts, which I think is pretty normal for everyone. Living on one income in this world is fucking tough. It's so tough that there is an entire chapter devoted to it. And when things don't go your way, and the bills pile up, I want to stay in bed all day or punch trees. I don't know why I want to punch trees, but there you go.

**Low testosterone.** You know what, I've got nothing to say about this. Go see a doctor. Get your levels checked, my man!

As a stay-at-home dad, you can't ignore these things. In all seriousness, we all need to take an active approach to protecting our mental health. It's tough because as men, we tend to internalize the process and the feelings. We think we can walk it off or rub some dirt on it. And as much as I love rubbing dirt all over things, it doesn't work very well. In fact, it's pretty dumb.

The problem is that some of our mental health concerns are really hard to pinpoint in behaviors. It's more than feeling "blue." It's being lethargic and disconnected. It's anger and frustration for no reason. It's having a short fuse when you damn well know you shouldn't. So, before I get into how to manage those risk factors, let's be clear. If you need help, go get fucking help. If I were near you, I would be yelling this. This is serious, and the time of hiding our inner shit is over. It doesn't work and makes us worse fathers. I've known tons of dads who have suffered from depression, and I applaud all of them who went and got help. And those who were open about it so the rest of us could learn, you guys are fucking heroes.

Now let's see if we can manage some of those risk factors. This doesn't always work, but taking positive steps from day one at least gives you a chance to succeed. And that's all you need, just the chance. Let's get to it. More lists, this time in the form of A, B, C because I'm running out of ways to present lists. I'm going to put *Expert List Maker* on my résumé.

## Because Dad Says So . . .

*For me, music is a huge therapy. I can just let go of thoughts and sing/dance around the house. I'm not good at dancing and it's pretty cringe but it's my release. Getting moving and getting the blood pumping is a good dopamine/endorphin release. It makes me smile naturally when sometimes I really have to force it. My son gets*

*excited and he starts dancing around with me and that
makes me smile even more. I will dance to* Bubble Guppies
*songs for hours with him.*

**David, father of one**


**A. Take the three a.m. feeding.** Yup, you should 100
percent be doing this with a new baby. First off, Mom does
appreciate the break from the boob monster. Second, you
know who is up at three a.m.? Fucking no one. And that
means it's all you. Every scream, cry, and poopy diaper is
all yours. All those glorious mistakes that you are going to
make? All on your shoulders. But slowly you'll realize
something: This is awesome. Yes, you're tired. But you're
also learning that you don't need anyone to rescue you.
The baby is crying? You've got this because you've been
training every night for three months. Dirty diaper? You
now carry a stopwatch and could match your skills with
the best. Two-handed diaper changes? Noob league.
And there is no one to cluck over you and take the baby
out of your arms. By the end of this, you will have gained
confidence. Everyone will come to you for advice because
you've lived the trial by fire. And if you want to watch
every episode of every version of *Star Trek*? Knock yourself
out. This is your bonding time, so use it. All three of my
kids can do the "live long and prosper" sign of the Vulcans.
They have no idea who the Kardashians are. I kick ass.

**B. Seek out sunlight.** Some of the best advice I got in the
beginning was to keep doors and blinds open as much as
possible. Let that light in. When I don't do it, I feel

trapped, and if it happens for a long enough time, I start to get a bit paranoid.

**C. Get out of the house.** This is my main mantra. Just because we are called stay-at-home dads doesn't mean we actually are there a ton. If I'm doing it right, every day I'm out of the house even if it is for a short bit. I get around people. I don't have to always talk to someone, but I need to be out. It can be a trip to the grocery store or library on my lazy days. Every single day. If I'm not breathing fresh air, it messes with me. Taking a walk around the block or even just sitting on the porch in winter jackets. Whatever. Get out of the house.

**D. Be connected to the community.** This is why I went into a whole chapter about dads groups, friends, and online support. Those are the guys who really understand what this is like. Check in with the guys and reach out. Lurk if you want to, it's all good.

**E. Be invested in your marriage.** I'm going to get into this much more later on, but for now, realize that when you are in the grind and shit is literally everywhere, it's easy to forget about your significant other. Don't get lost and forget why you do this. Yes, it's for the children, but think bigger. It's for your family, and that starts with your marriage. So actively participate in it, and plan nights out or walks with just the two of you.

**F. Get an interest.** It doesn't have to be a hobby, but it has to be something that is only for you. Something that you can lose yourself in for a while without thinking about anyone's problems. It helps to remind you that you are more than the guy who makes sandwiches and cleans urine. For me, I play chess, read, and do woodworking. I also game with my son or by myself. I make time for these activities. And my wife realizes that it's not me "screwing around." She knows that this is how I actively take care of my mental health.

**G. Go solo.** One night a month, at a minimum, take off. Go see a movie by yourself. Do you know how cheap it is to go see a movie with just you? Compared to the sixty bucks when I take the family, it's a steal. My point is, get away from the chaos and let someone else handle it. Take your day off.

**H. Weekend is family time.** Now that you've had time alone, make time for the entire family to do things together. Yes, there will be chores, but your life is more than just chores. Go to the park together, take a hike in the woods, whatever. Your weekends are for family fun time. It's how you all grow closer together, and you desperately need all these people. They are your garden; water them with fun. That's a good metaphor. Grow your garden, damn it.

**I. Get mental health checkups.** Every once in a while, schedule some sit-down time with a therapist. Maybe you don't need it. Maybe you're so stoic that you should be in a 1960s western. But it never hurts to get a checkup. Just like you would with a medical doctor, go talk to a professional. Think of it as getting a tune-up on your car. That's what your head is, an engine. Go get it checked out every once in a while.

### Because Dad Says So . . .

*I volunteer. Giving back is a great way to keep your mental health up, along with some serious reality checks along the way. Whether I'm working with kids or adults, helping others achieve their goals is a great way to beat the blues. I was the point man for a bake sale at the kids' school that raised over $800 for military family scholarships.*

**Everett Lopez, father of one**

There are a lot more strategies to combating depression and managing those risk factors. Look online or get a book and pay attention to it. This is an abbreviated list, and not everything on it may work for you, but you need to try. Set yourself up for a win. A lot of these things that I do have become habits, and habits start with repetitive action.

### FROM THE DADS GROUP

**MICK:** Did I do a good job of watching out for my mental health? I don't think so. Sometimes, things just got so busy and I didn't feel like I was doing things well. I took up gardening and that helped and gave me time to think. Admitting that you have faults though and not trying to be perfect is where my head usually went.

**LARRY:** I have a high tolerance for crap, but winter is tough on everyone. The days are shorter and there's less time, but you still have all the responsibilities. I'm an introvert but even I found that getting out of the house was important. It doesn't have to be a big deal or a huge adventure. It could be a walk by yourself.

**JAKE:** I enjoy getting together with everyone, but it just leaves me wiped out. Physically and emotionally, I'm just done. I don't typically enjoy large groups of people. Keeping a good schedule helps me know what to expect and also plan my time away from crowds and people. It allows me to recharge.

**MIKE:** Find something that is yours and only yours. Switch gears in your head when you get to it and leave the guilt behind. Having something that can take you out of the moment of parenting, something where you are looking after your own needs, helps with staying alert and fresh.

# AND NOW SOME ANXIETY TIPS, BROUGHT TO YOU BY CONSTANT WORRY!

It makes me anxious when I sit around the house and realize that I don't have anxiety. Son of a bitch. It's a self-fulfilling cycle. *Oh, I feel great today! You won't tomorrow! Shit.* Luckily, I have the ability to make fun of everything, and that helps.

Right now, I have more list anxiety. Will this list be as good as the last list? Does the list do its intended job of conveying information quickly so you don't get bogged down? Should I name my child List? Welcome to the inner workings of my head. Shit gets weird.

And please don't think I'm making light of people who have any of the many, many forms of anxiety. Just remember that I have to make jokes, or all this would be so overwhelming that I would never leave the house.

Have I used Roman numerals in a list yet? I don't think so! Great, here is your highly qualified Roman-numeraled list on how to proactively help with anxiety.

**I. Practice list consistency.** When you make lists, try to number them the same so you don't sit down at your desk for hours debating A, B, C or 1, 2, 3 for the order of lists. I've spent way more time on this than I should have.

**II. Put yourself into time-out.** Hell yes! This is a thing and completely okay to do. My three-year-old niece, Sidda, put me into time-out once because "Uncle Shannon makes bad decisions." Apparently, I have a bit of a potty mouth. Turns out, though, this is one of the greatest things you can do for yourself. When the pressure gets too much, or your patience is turning into anger, separate yourself. Go somewhere quiet. Set a timer if you have to. It's okay not to be "on" all the freaking time, and taking ten minutes a couple of times a day is good for you. Do it. It really does help.

**III. Eat and sleep well.** See Chapter 2 about eating. As for sleep, get your eight hours in if you can. I know that for us as parents, this seems to be a pipe dream, especially if you are doing the late-night feedings. But when you can, make sure you are well rested. It really does get better. I know that if I don't sleep well, I'm risking my behavior for tomorrow. This is tough, as many of us also know that the only time we have to ourselves is at night. Find a happy medium and stick to it. At the very least, nap when your kids nap.

## Because Dad Says So . . .

*I use a sensory deprivation tank, more commonly known as a float tank. The water and air temperature are the same as your body and you wear earplugs. It gives me the feeling of weightlessness. Not only does it relieve all the pressure on my body, but it also allows me to clear my mind and meditate. After an hour, I'm all refreshed and my wife notices a huge difference in my mood, and I'm generally a lot calmer.*

**Matthew Holm, father of one**

**IV. Exercise.** Nothing feels better than a rage workout. It helps with that extra energy I get from anxiety. In fact, I went through a bad breakup in college, and lifting weights while cussing at them helped a ton. Now I just cuss silently on long walks. I may look a little like the crazy man on the street, but it gives me an outlet for that frustration that turns into anxiety.

**V. Meditate.** I got this advice from another dad, and my first thought was *Yeah, whatever, hippie.* Then I did it and I now need to go apologize to that dad. What I have found is that it helps me redirect the negative thoughts I'm having and organize my brain for the rest of the day. There, I can get control of those emotions or at least acknowledge them before they become overwhelming. Try it to help break those thought patterns that seem to escalate.

**VI. Give up on perfection.** This is Mick's advice that is so good, I'm going to claim it as my own. You don't always have to match that guy in your head. You don't have to be perfect. You need to accept this very early on. You do not have control of everything you think you have control over.

**VII. Humor!** This is, obviously, my go-to. A well-placed joke or something silly has a way of breaking the tension. Not only in public, but in my own head as well. It helps me see the absurdity of my own thoughts, which helps me put them in proper context.

**VIII. Learn your triggers.** This is going to take some time and some honest answers. If you can figure out what sets you off, what starts your negative thoughts, you can learn to manage those things. For me, it took a therapist. But I know what my triggers are and how to break the cycle of negative or obsessive thoughts. It takes some time, but it's worth it.

**IX. Get your someone.** For me, having someone that I can talk to about what's in my head has a way of defusing the thoughts. Mostly it's my wife but it's also my fellow dads. And when I do talk about my worries or anxiety with Erin, she puts her hand on my forearm and squeezes. This helps me when the anxiety is peaking. It takes a while to work, but it always does. Hearing the anxious thoughts out loud has a way of making them more manageable. Find your someone. Open up. It's uncomfortable, but there are real benefits to being that vulnerable.

## Because Dad Says So . . .

*I need time to declutter my mind. I have OCD to begin with, so it takes me a long time to unwind in normal circumstances. I have a perfectionist's mind that needs to feel at rest before I can sleep. Reading and exercise help me do that. I take a four-mile walk every day at lunchtime and listen to audiobooks for that hour.*

**Ryan Scarola, father of one**

Of course, we all go through more than what is mentioned here. This isn't meant to be an all-inclusive list of every issue that we dads face. These are just the most common. So, think of yourself as the prom king of mental health. And the advice I've given is from my own experience, where I've learned what works for me.

I urge you, more than any other piece of advice, to find a professional to deal with this stuff. It's heavy and uncomfortable to talk about. When we do, we often feel that we are going to be ridiculed. Out of everything I've ever written, this has been the hardest. Not only because it is the most honest, but also because

I don't feel deserving. I don't know why. I've certainly been down these roads for a long enough period of time, but at the same time, I feel exposed when I talk about my own fucked-up issues.

So where can you go to get help? Movember is a great place to start. Movember is the leading advocate that focuses on men's health, and that includes mental health. They run a campaign every November to bring attention to the issues that men face, such as suicide and depression. We all grow our 'staches out and then twirl them because that's cool. At Movember you can get advice from guys who not only know what it's like to be hurting, but guys who know where to get help. Start with their website, and it'll direct you to helpful resources.

Next, I know that finding a therapist can be hard. In the US, try going to *Psychology Today*. Through its website, you can search for a therapist based on a ton of different filters, from orientation and gender to area of expertise. You can also search based on zip code as well as cost. If you don't have health insurance that covers therapy, there are many that work on a sliding scale, and it's more affordable than you think.

Then make the call for an appointment, which I know can be tough. My confession here? I wouldn't have done it without Erin. Making that call to schedule an appointment was a roadblock. At Erin's suggestion, I wrote a script down because honestly I couldn't even frame what I needed help with. It was just a way to clarify my thoughts and give a general idea. I had to call around a bit as some therapists weren't taking patients, so I'm thankful for the script to keep me on task. Give it a shot, it really does help. And don't worry if you can't find the right words to say about what's going on in your head. Keep it simple: I'm feeling off and I'm not sure why. It would help to have someone to talk to.

If I can do this, then so can you. Get the help you deserve, and then come tell the rest of us how you did it. That's a victory I want to celebrate.

---

## FROM THE DADS GROUP

**MICK:** Stop the self-criticism circle. Recognize your patterns, the things that you know set you off, and make a plan on how to deal with them or avoid them before you start.

**LARRY:** My to-do list can get pretty big. And when something needs to be done, and I don't want to do it, that's when I find myself losing a little composure. My wife, Jane, is good about stepping in at that moment and taking things off my plate. And sometimes it's calling my friends and getting some help.

**JAKE:** What's the next step, that's what I always think when everything gets overwhelming. Break it down into smaller things. Get that done, refresh, and keep going.

**MIKE:** Every situation is different, and you should treat it as such. What works for one may not work for another, and that includes people. So, take stock of yourself and know when to walk away. Trust your partner to take care of what you don't have the energy for. You're a team.

## YOUR RELATIONSHIP

If the first part of this chapter was awkward, wait until you get to this one. Ya know, for some reason, most of us at-home dads don't talk about our marriage in any public sense. I mean, I know my dad friends are married, but a good 60 percent of the time, I probably couldn't tell you what the wife's name is. And if you asked me what she does for a living, I would probably make something up. For example, Amanda (Mike's wife) I think does something related to drug cartels. I mean, I wouldn't swear on it, but I like the thought of Amanda reading this and giving Mike shit for choosing bad friends. I'm joking. Amanda is in marketing. Kelly (Mick's wife) works for the mob, though. Don't tell anyone.

As you can imagine, being an at-home dad brings a whole different set of stressors to a marriage. You and your family are ditching the traditional roles. That is going to bring some new problems to your doorstep or reframe old ones.

I'm not a trained counselor, please keep that in mind. But I have done this for a long time and have seen the pitfalls that a lot of guys trip into. At the very least, I can share the things that I have seen and how they have affected other dads in the same situation, or what I have encountered in my own relationship with my wife. And if you are having a hard time, just keep in mind that Amanda probably works for a traveling circus as well as the drug cartel.

To start with, I'm going to pass on the best piece of advice I have ever received as an at-home dad. I'm pretty sure this is a bumper sticker somewhere, but it's solid, and when I look at my marriage through this lens and at the stress that being an at-home dad puts on it, I'm able to reframe my thoughts.

When there is a problem, whether the water heater is broken or the house isn't clean, remember that it's not you versus your significant other versus the problem. It's **you and your spouse versus the problem**, whatever that happens to be. Start with that in mind. Make it your mantra as you chant your way through yet another mindless *Spy Kids* movie. Also, please stop making those. I can't take it anymore.

Next, remember that the decision for you to stay home with the kids wasn't your choice alone. You and your spouse had to come to this decision together. It doesn't feel like it sometimes when you are covered in baby vomit, but it's true. And if you both haven't bought into this with 100 percent conviction and dedication, you are going to have problems. This is not a decision that you can make unilaterally, and one partner cannot be on the fence about it. Things can get really bad really quick if that is the case. This is your foundation, and if you don't have it, don't become an at-home dad. That's harsh advice, but this is important enough that it needs to be said bluntly.

Finally, before we get to another list, each of you needs to have empathy for the other. You probably know what it's like to be the sole income provider and the pressure that it brings. Your spouse almost certainly knows what's it's like to be judged by other parents constantly. Empathy is your greatest asset as a couple. See the world from your partner's eyes, and it will help with your own frustrations.

> **DAD HACK**
>
> When your spouse gets home, do not assume you are off. Do not throw the kids at her. Give her thirty minutes of free time where she can collect herself and settle in after a long day. Make this an everyday habit and expect the same in return. This is parenting; you are never off. Continue to act as if she is not there.

**Communication and expectations.** This is one of those yelling and screaming pieces of advice I need to give to make sure you get the point. You and your significant other must have clear and total communication about everything. Money, sex, the daily grind—all of it. And this needs to happen every fucking day. And while you are doing all that great communication, continue to set specific expectations. Don't attack each other when there is a problem or an issue. Work through the problem together.

## Because Dad Says So . . .

*A lot of times, it is my wife that will recognize my stress signs and will gently tug on strings until I can pinpoint what is bothering me. Other times, I can just come out with it, blundering and guy-like. I have not found the magical phrase that works well with everything, but understanding each other helps.*

**Robert Burnell, father of two**

**Let your spouse find their own way with the kids.** This piece of advice actually comes from a mom I knew years ago. Don't play the hero when your partner is with the kids. Let them figure out their own system, their own schedule, and their own way of doing things. It's eas to say, "Well, I do it this way," but that just makes you look like a dick. They are a parent as much as you are. Back off and enjoy your break.

**Feeling unappreciated.** This is universal and it happens on both sides. There are times when you feel like you are carrying all the weight. Conversely, your spouse will feel the exact same thing at the exact same time. The question becomes, how do you deal with it before things get angry? Make it a point to be their cheerleader. Give them that positive reinforcement that they are doing a great job as a partner. Thank them for doing the small things. Every dad I know has been there. And don't worry, we are going to flip it when I talk to the moms because that shit is going to happen.

**Decompress together at the end of the day.** This isn't my advice, but something given to me by one of the other guys in my group a long time ago. Each night, he and his wife would go to bed together, even if he wasn't tired. He would sit and listen to her day and vice versa. They would make plans for the next day. They would work on any problems together. I have taken this as gospel. I have so much advertising jargon in my head from listening to my wife. I have no idea what it means, it's so industry specific, but I know that the RFP needs to get done quick and if Jim doesn't get his ass in gear, shit's going to get real. Good luck, Jim. I have no idea who you are, but you fucking owe me for talking her off the cliff.

**Quarterly reviews.** This is going to be the toughest piece of advice I have to give in the book. For the first year at least, you and your significant other need to sit down and see how things are going every three months. Make sure the kids are nowhere near you; this is not a conversation to have while nuggets are being thrown at your head. Are you both happy with the result? Is there any resentment building? Can you do this financially? Is there something that needs to be done better on either side? Are you both still all the way in? If not, you need to quit. There, I said it. Your marriage and your family are more important. The whole premise of how to be an at-home dad is to do what works for your family. If this isn't working for both of you and the children, stop. It's such a simple thing to say but it's so hard to do.

---

### FROM THE DADS GROUP

**MICK:** I have a quote pinned up in my house that does a pretty good job of reminding me how to make it through marriage. It's by Thornton Wilder. "I didn't marry you because you were perfect. I didn't even marry you because I loved you. I married you because you gave me a promise." I keep that as a reminder. It's a promise that I made to my wife and to my God and I take it seriously. Remembering that makes other things seem easier.

**LARRY:** There isn't really a definition of what we consider the usual gender roles. Dishes don't care who washes them. With less-defined roles, it makes it easier to take each job as it comes up and to divide the tasks. Everyone is pitching in around the house and that's the way it should be. Work together as a team. Those are the expectations we have set.

**JAKE:** Don't score keep against your spouse. What I mean is, recognize that your partner is doing her part and you're doing yours. And if you're both in all the way, there is no reason to ask who is doing more.

**MIKE:** Every Sunday night, my wife and I will talk about what the next week looks like. We plan then together. We do this constantly. It keeps us on the same page and keeps the stress down. So, I guess it's our communication and always being open with each other that has helped us manage our life and protect our marriage.

# HI, MOMS, LET'S HAVE A CHAT

All right, Dads, take a break. I've told you time and time again that this whole thing works better with communication. Part of that is being able to ask for help. But that sucks and no one likes doing it, so I'm going to do it for you.

Tear these pages out of the book and hand them over to your significant other. Or just give them the whole book, but you will feel way manlier if you tear them out. Flex a little while you do it. Damn, that's impressive. Now hand the pages to your significant other, and I'll take it from there. Stand back, I'm about to score you some free doughnuts.

Hi, Moms. We need to have a little chat.

You don't know me, but my name is Shannon. I'm a dad. I have a girl's name, which makes me kinda cool in a "Boy Named Sue" way. It's okay to be impressed. I was once named one of the Funniest Women of the Week by *BuzzFeed*. That's a true story. As is the fact that I also once scored a free year's subscription to *Cosmo* for my wife.

Anyway, your guy is becoming the ultimate stay-at-home dad by reading this book. To get there, he needs your help, but help isn't easy to ask for. It's weird and awkward so I'm going to do it for him.

First off, your world has changed or is about to change once your guy becomes an at-home dad, and we need to talk about that. Things aren't as simple as we would like them to be. He's going to catch shit from time to time about his choice to stay home with the kids. It's cool, I'm teaching him how to deal with that.

But you are going to catch some grief for it as well.

Let's get all the cards on the table. I'm writing this chapter with the help of some moms. The moms from my dads group. See, it's not just a dads group, not really. It's more of a parents group at this point. And I'll be joined by five very funny and knowledgeable women that can relate to what you are going through.

On occasion in the world, someone is going to make a comment such as "You let him stay home with the kids?" My advice, as a dad and a guy, is to feel free to punch these people in the face. However, the moms I talked to don't think that is a very good idea.

Their recommendation instead is to answer that your husband doesn't need anyone's permission to stay home with his kids. He's a parent, for Pete's sake. What the hell?!

With mommy wars and debates on whether you should stay home or go to work, you get a lot of shit. So it shouldn't surprise you that you're going to get crap for this as well. I'm sorry. I'll tell you the same thing that I told the dads: Screw those people. You are doing what is best for your family. Period. There is no need to justify yourself to anyone, so don't.

All right. After the punching, let's move on to how to support your husband. This is a dad book, after all, so we are going to go over some things to make it a bit easier to avoid some problems that some dads have trouble with. Some of it will be hard advice, but it works. And it's not just mine; I've gone over all this with the moms who are the sole providers for their families. They understand the stress that can be on your shoulders. You should absolutely listen to them.

1. **Being different doesn't mean wrong.** Understand that he needs to find his own way. He's going to learn, and eventually there will be times where he does things differently than the way you would do it. You need to back down. Dads and moms parent differently. His way is not always wrong, and your way isn't always right. It's just different. If he has a different system in place than you did or would, be okay with that. Don't argue about it. He's doing this all the time. He's got this. Don't swoop in and rescue him. He doesn't need it.

2. **Practice positive reinforcement.** You are both going to get to the point where you feel unappreciated. You are going to feel that you are doing all the heavy lifting by going to work every day. He's going to feel the same way. He's going to be knee-deep in puke and poop and wondering why he isn't getting help. It doesn't matter if you are helping and it doesn't matter if he has a side gig to bring in money. Eventually, we all have those moments where we feel like we are doing everything. My best advice is to tell him that he's doing a good job, or that you liked the dinner, or that you love seeing him do so well. It's a minor thing, to be sure, but it does make a difference in our own mental health. And yup, I've told him the same thing.

3. **Take built-in breaks.** Everyone needs a break, and you need to recognize this from the start. His day doesn't end when you get home, he just gets a little bit of help. He's not going to throw the kids at you and make a break for the door either. You get your downtime. You need to give it to him as well. Take over a task, such as the bathing or bedtime, and let your at-home husband chill. Give him some time each week when he can do something without the kids. He needs it. He won't ask for it, though, so you've got to bring it up.

4. **Schedule mental health check-ins.** This one is from my wife. Her name is Erin. You'd like her, although she has a strict no-punching-in-the-face policy. Erin checks in on how I'm feeling and pays attentions to my peaks and valleys. I have found that I love the fact that she is thinking about me because, honestly, most of us ignore our own mental health. Don't let him. There are some

days where I don't believe anyone is thinking about how I'm doing. I'll have a baby on my hip and applesauce in my beard. It can get very lonely and isolating. Check in on his mental health, and make sure he gets professional help when he needs it.

5. **Take one thing and make it yours.** Maybe you are the one who makes all the doctors' appointments. Now, you may be saying, "But I work, this is all his stuff!" And my response would be to ask, "How are you at changing tires?" Maybe you're an expert at mowing the lawn and small tractor repair. Because the truth of the at-home-dad gig is that we have to do all the normal dad stuff and maintenance, plus all the other home duties. The division of work isn't really as separated as you would think from the traditional roles. I still have a honey-do list. Take something off his plate and make it yours. Just because you work doesn't mean you aren't a parent. And yup, feel free to yell that some working husbands aren't helping enough at home, too. That's some bullshit.

6. **Be all-in.** This is the best advice I can give you, and this doesn't come just from me. This is from the moms again. If you aren't 100 percent on board with your husband being an at-home dad, you can't do this. Resentment is a real thing, and this causes trouble in marriages. I've seen it. The moms say that you have to have a strong foundation before even considering this move because it is fraught with difficulties. That means you need to clearly give him your expectations from the start and listen to his. Without that foundation, things can go pretty sour over time. You are a team. It's you and your husband versus the

problem, not the problem versus him. Recognize that at the beginning. Be all-in or don't do this at all.

7. **Buy the man a doughnut.** That's just good life advice.

Okay, here are the moms of my dads group. They are going to chime in here about how to support your stay-at-home dad and take care of yourself. Oh, and also don't refer to us as "house husbands." We hate that shit. Don't do it, please. Or Mr. Mom. That's crap as well. You know what, just call us Dad. That's cool.

## FROM THE MOMS

**KELLY:** There is some stress to being the sole bread-winner and knowing that your option to quit isn't on the table as much as it might have been. And for us, this isn't tied to gender. It brings an understanding to both of us of the other's perspective. Mick understands the pressure I'm under and supports me. My goal with him is to let him know how much I appreciate all that he does and that I realize how hard it is to be the stay-at-home parent. He's under different pressures and it's important that he knows that I recognize that.

**JANE:** You have to have that mutual level of trust in each other. There is a lot of pressure that society puts on all of us. Ignore it and trust in your partner. He will find his way and it's going to be different from yours. Embrace him for that.

**AMY:** I'm an organizer and Jake is more go with the flow. Pick your battles and understand each other's weaknesses and strengths. Don't fight against them. Instead, recognize what you are both good at and then back off and let him do his thing. He's got this. As for our marriage, our strength as a couple is that we take time for our relationship. We put other things on hold and make it a priority through all the busyness of parenting. Date nights, spending time together after kids are in bed, etc. That and being able to make each other laugh. Both were hugely important when the kids were little.

AMANDA: Practice patience with your spouse and yourself. I had to rethink my expectations of how things were done in the beginning. Encourage him to take time for himself in little and big ways. From dad nights out or watching TV uninterrupted to weekends away, we both need time to step away from parenting and adulting. Mike has three sacred weekends each year, and we respect that time from a scheduling and family budget perspective. We make sure they happen no matter what else is going on.

ERIN: My response to everything is 100 percent "flight" and Shannon's is "fight," except for June bugs. He flees from them like a cat escaping bath time. Because I know his reflex is to fight any negative situation, internal or external, it means I know when something is bothering him often before he does. He paces, fidgets, is short-tempered and grumpy; the opposite of his usual demeanor.

When I notice these changes, I know it's time to take him to a quiet part of the house—away from the kids, responsibilities, and noise—and ask him what's wrong. He usually doesn't know right away, but we get there eventually. Maybe he is being pulled in too many directions, or he can't focus, or maybe it's because it's been rainy for several days and it makes

> him feel like jumping out of his skin. Being able to see
> him, his quirks and tics, all for better or worse, allows
> me to offer him the unconditional support he needs.
> Sometimes it's a kick in the ass and other times it's a
> hug. Pay attention to your significant other's unspo-
> ken communication and recognize when they need
> help, because often they aren't going to ask for it.

## OTHER RELATIONSHIPS

Welcome back, Dads! Now we get to the fun part—watching
other people freak out when they find out that you're an at-home
dad. Honestly, I live for this shit.

Do they really freak out? No, not most of them. Most people
you will encounter out in the wild will simply nod their heads
and treat you like a normal person. Others, like certain individuals at the park who are named Karen, may accuse you of being
creepy because you're at the park and they don't see your kid.
Nobody really likes her, even the moms. But most people are
pretty cool and the comments you get are innocent.

"Oh, are you babysitting today?" is a family favorite, as is
"Giving Mom the day off?" When I encounter these, I tend to
just let it go or offer a "Nope, I do this full time" and leave it at
that. When people say this, it's not meant as an insult, and honestly, who's got time to deal with that every day? I try to simplify
my life as much as possible. It's usually a grandma at the grocery
store, and as long as she has butterscotch candy, I'm good to go.
My advice on these casual encounters is to play it cool and either

smile or own it. Educate rather than berate. I'm going to make that into a bumper sticker.

Then there are the people you see regularly but for whom it hasn't sunk in that you're the primary caregiver. These situations are a little bit trickier. For example, how do you tell the receptionist at the pediatrician's office to call you first rather than your wife when the strep throat results are in?

Here's my answer.

I have no fucking idea. I've been dealing with this shit for twelve years and they still call my wife. Every time I show up to the doctor's, if it's a new receptionist, I have to make it a point to tell her my number is first in the charts and I need to be called before my wife. She smiles, says no problem, and then promptly calls my wife to ask if it's okay that her husband is here with the children.

As for preschools and elementary schools, there is an answer for that one. You have to be a "known" quantity. That is, you have to show up all the time and be chatty. Crack the dad jokes, volunteer for everything, and participate in whatever the school has got going on. I can craft some serious cotton-ball snowmen, just saying. You have to be around for a while before everyone considers you harmless, which is weird. At that point, most likely they will stop with the comments and actually call you first. This is the process of being vetted, which happens to us dads quite a bit. Roll with it, let them get to know you, and be active and involved.

Moving on to family members. This is my favorite part because I do love awkward Thanksgivings.

There may be some in your clan who don't exactly agree with what you do, which is weird because I don't remember asking for permission. But be that as it may, you might catch shit from some of your more old-school family members. Most have this vision in their head of what a man is supposed to be and supposed to do. It usually involves not going to the doctor for a torn-off leg.

Family relationships can be difficult, I get it. How do you handle those snide comments?

First off, there is nothing that says you have to be anyone's whipping boy. You don't have to be polite. In fact, I encourage you not to. Who likes being piled on? I'm not saying that you should be a complete dick either, but you shouldn't be silent. This is who you are. Take the approach of "Do no harm but take no shit."

You are not asking for anyone's acceptance. Who needs that? You've got two million other guys cheering you on. More than that, you have your immediate family. That's whose opinion really matters. No one else's. This is what I mean by owning it. At-home dads do not make excuses for what we do, even if others want us to. I'm not unemployable, Gene. Eat a dick.

If they make snide comments, tell them the truth. "I didn't know it was so controversial to love and support your children. That really explains why your daughter has daddy issues."

Okay, wait. That was still pretty dickish. Let's try that again. Maybe with a mother-in-law this time.

"Thanks for your concern about my family's well-being. I will keep your opinion in mind the next time your daughter and I are making you another grandkid. Can we borrow your car?"

Wait. Wait. Wait. That's pretty dickish, too. Okay, last try. Let's do a reasonable response to the constant attacks at your manhood.

Ahem.

"Fuck off."

For the record, that last one makes for some great Thanksgiving drama. But seriously, engage the person who keeps making those comments. Do it calmly and without anger (if you can after a while). Then tell them point-blank, "I'm an at-home dad. I don't regret it. I love being there for my children and seeing our family grow. If you can accept that, that would be great. If you can't, well, that's more a problem that you have and not me. From now on, you can keep your comments to yourself."

There, that's a solid answer. But then tell them to fuck off.

Don't let people who are close to you push you around. You don't need their approval. You've already won at life. You're a dad to some great kids. They say these things because of their own insecurities. So, whether it's a brother-in-law or your own blood family, just tell the truth. Tell them why you do it. Then stand up for yourself and tell them to knock that off.

The truth of it is that most family members will love you even more for taking care of your kids. The two greatest men I have ever known, my father and grandfather, loved the fact that I'm an at-home dad. They were my biggest supporters, and both grew up in some very old-time ways. Both were in wars. Both were as tough as men come. And both knew the value of being there for your children. I am what I am because they gave me that confidence. Most of your family will be like this, and that's why they are family.

However . . .

If you want to be passive-aggressive about it, because it's fun, then maybe the next time a nice summer Tuesday morning rolls around, you start sending them a shit ton of pics of you at the pool. Make sure you ask them how the traffic was on their drive into work that day. After that, offer to give them some family pictures of the kids that they can hang on the felt walls of their drab cubicle. But only if their boss is okay with it. You don't want anyone getting into trouble. If they have to work late again, let them know that eventually they will have time to see your kids, probably around high school.

Full disclosure—I have actually done this. No regrets.

## FROM THE DADS GROUP

**MICK:** If it's a family member, I tell them that people take care of those close to them in different ways. Do I wish they would accept it? Yes, of course I do. Is it going to change anything about how I feel about what I do? Nope.

**LARRY:** When we are out in the group, it seemed that I got asked if we were babysitting way more often than when I was alone. My response was always "Nope, being a dad," and then I would walk way. For family, I have said, "Oh yeah, how about we trade jobs for a few days," and that was usually the end of it.

**JAKE:** With internet trolls, I used to get angry and pick a fight. Nowadays I don't have time or the energy for even interacting with them. It's a waste of time. So, I just mock them and move on.

**MIKE:** It's not often that I get much grief about being an at-home dad. But when it does happen, I'm always quick to point out that my kids and my wife come first. They would turn and walk away, and I would mutter under my breath for them to go fuck themselves.

## YOUR OWN SELF-WORTH

We have to get back into your own head again. Why? Well, because this whole chapter has been leading up to this next part. Send me some passive-aggressive text messages if it will make you feel better.

Sooner or later, you are truly going to wrestle with your self-worth and it's going to be hard. I'm not talking about how it is in the beginning when you transition from working dad to primary caregiver. I'm talking about when it's been a year or so and you start thinking about your future. It's tough to see your contributions to the family and it's natural for us to question it. I don't know an at-home dad who hasn't had to go through this. Hell, my own dads-group dads are confident as shit and we've all struggled with this question.

I'm not talking about working or not working. I'm not going back into how others view you and how that affects you. We've dealt with all that. No, this one is man versus self. That's where this self-worth struggle comes from. And I'll be honest, it's not easy.

When you work, you have a paycheck that validates the things you do. You get promotions and certificates of appreciation. You get to buy a new car or not freak out when the water heater needs to be replaced. All those add up to a feeling that you are worth something to your family, to yourself. When you stay home with the kids, there are no concrete positive reinforcements like that. They are elusive.

The reason that those snide comments people make don't bother me is because I've said way worse to myself. I've had those thoughts. What am I really providing to the family? What are they getting out of this? If I can't make this house perfect, what am I actually worth? Am I really a lazy bastard that is unemployable? What the ever-loving fuck am I doing?

My head is a very weird place sometimes. What I'm trying to tell you is that I've been through those times when I don't think I'm worth much to my family. Therefore, I'm not much worth to myself.

Those are some fucking dark times. And every at-home dad at one point or another has struggled with them. It's how we deal with them that matters. It's difficult, though, when the only positive reinforcement comes from a little person not throwing applesauce at the dog.

You don't have to be perfect. You need to get that right into your head as soon as possible and be okay with it. No parent knows what they are doing. Once you've been around for a while and see enough parents, you will realize, the same as I did, that we are all pretty much winging it. And those who seem to have all their shit together, with their perfect homes and perfect smiles, are usually screwed up as well. They are asking themselves the same question you are: What is my self-worth? You can look at me and see the same thing, but by now you know the struggles I've been through and that some days I'm just barely holding it together. And other days, I'm not holding anything down. I'm very far from perfect. And yet, I dig me.

With that in mind, we can employ a couple of strategies to truly see how much you are worth.

Look at your family. Look at your kids. Are they thriving? That's the first place I look every time I need to validate that I made the right decision. I look at the relationship I have with them. When someone needs a hug, I'm the first guy they come to. When someone is scared, it's my arms that they run for. I hold on to those everyday moments like a drowning man holds on to a life preserver.

The funny thing about my kids is that they all look exactly like my wife. They have her nose and thick hair. Their chins and cheeks are 100 percent my wife.

But every single one of them acts like me. I can see it every time my daughter accidentally smashes something. When my son gets lost in his facts, that's all me. When my youngest tries to punch the oldest, sadly, that's me. They joke like me and keep trying to take it further. And they embrace life like me. If you ask my kids if they would rather craft a fake turkey out of Popsicle sticks or build a guillotine, they will always choose a guillotine. Well, that's a bad example, because who wouldn't choose a guillotine?

When I look at my children, really observe when they don't know I'm watching, I see three little minions acting exactly like I act. They have parts of my personality. Nature versus nurture, who knows. But those three are me. That's my validation that I've done the right thing. When they read me their stories at night, or when they tell me an awkward joke, my heart fills with pride. I like me a lot. I love them.

I want you to try something else, as well. This is always very abstract, which can be tough. You need something to hold on to. Something to point at and say, "See, this is awesome. They are awesome."

In my house, I have something called the "adventure wall." It's the wall of the staircase. On this wall are the pictures of everything we have done. From the silly adventures to the time we built a trebuchet, they are all up there. Baby pictures of their first pumpkin carving or my son's first Halloween costume. There's the World's Largest Ball of Twine. The World's Largest Pair of Overalls. Every memory that we have documented over the years.

To get to bed every night, I have to walk by this wall. Without fail, I always pause for a second and look. That's my tangible validation. That adventure wall helps remind me that the choice I made so many years ago was the right choice. My kids will often comment on the pictures, reliving the memories that we have up there. They'll laugh and joke and give me the highlights. I remember every detail, but I love their stories and the way they tell them. The things that have stuck with them.

I did that.

That's where I get my self-worth from. Did I make the right decision to become an at-home dad? You're damn right I did.

## FROM THE DADS GROUP

Instead of each individual dad here telling you how they found their self-worth and how they know what they mean to their family, I wanted to let you know a few things. Our answer was the same. We know our self-worth because we can see it in our children and families. That's what it came down to. Even Mike decided not to be contrary.

But what was interesting was trying to get the other dads to verbalize what they felt inside. In fact, this whole chapter was a struggle for any of us to talk about. To quote Larry, "It's not that we can't answer these questions, it's just that these are very hard questions to answer." Even our group, as close as we are, have difficulty talking about these topics in front of other people or finding the words to do the subject justice.

To get their advice on this chapter, I got us all together, including the moms. I tried to lead a discussion, and many times it was the moms who were more comfortable talking about their husbands' mental health than the dads themselves were. Sometimes all I would get was a grunt. And although I am the master at interpreting Jake's grunts, I needed this chapter to be as clear as possible. This took hours, but eventually the guys opened up. This included me, who tried to find a dozen ways to NOT write all this down.

But I knew it was important, and if I couldn't admit these things on the page, how could I expect to help anyone? Know that if this group of fathers, the most competent guys I have ever seen, have struggles with this, then it's okay for you, too. I mean it when I say we aren't perfect. It's pretty much Mick's motto. But I also think Mick is way, way too hard on himself. He's handled situations that would have broken me. Mick is always a "do what's right" type of guy. Once he decides what that is, he is relentless. He doesn't tell anyone. He doesn't brag. He just does. That is a strength that I wish I had myself.

To finish, know that you have self-worth if only for the reason that your family, and all of us, believe that you do. And that's enough.

# CHAPTER 5

# DADVENTURES!

This is basically your paycheck and you cash it in with memories.

When it comes to adventuring with kids, I'm the guy you want next to you in the minivan. This is my specialty, and now you're all in the apprenticeship program.

Look, I know that staying home all the time can be appealing. It's safe and comfy. It's also boring as hell. I'm sure you've had thoughts of sitting around a nice clean home all day. Watching some TV, maybe having some video game time, and finishing up with cello lessons for your one-year-old. I know you have because I have as well.

When I first started staying at home, I made a study schedule for Vivi. She was nineteen months old and Wyatt was a newborn. I figured that by the time Vivi turned two, she would be reading. By age three, math genius. At four there would really be no need for school as I was doing a fine job on my own. And the house would be clean, dinner would be great, and oh my God I would be so fulfilled! Maybe I could teach her curling! Do I do curling? Nope, but I'm a great teacher.

Yeah, that didn't work. I crashed and burned so hard in the beginning that I cringe now. Within a week, I was covered in vomit, the dog was covered in vomit, and newborn Wyatt was covered in vomit. It wasn't even our puke, it all belonged to Vivi. I was so tired that I would close my eyes while folding laundry, using the repetitive nature of the action as almost a lullaby. Then boom, vomit-palooza.

Somewhere in the beginning, my mind went numb. I was bored. There was no mental stimulation. There were no friendships. There was absolutely no adventuring. A month in and I started counting the popcorn on the ceiling. Yes, I did that. I even had a grid system.

I thought, *Ha, this would be funny, wouldn't it? I can write about this and make it a joke!* I devised a grid pattern, and before I knew it, I was taking it seriously and had forgotten it was supposed to be for a laugh. I shook it off and went outside. A police car rolled by, and hand to God, I thought, *Are they here for me?* I kid you not, that's the thought that went through my head. I was convinced someone had reported that some strange dude was in the house alone with kids. That's messed up, but that's what staying inside the house does to you. It messes with your head.

My new dads, you're finding excuses for why never to leave the house right now because I did the exact same thing.

"No! I am perfectly fine staying home all day every day. I'm an introvert. This is what introverts do! I've got this," I said to myself.

I did not have this, and I am not an introvert.

I was a wreck, and I hadn't realized one of the biggest benefits of being a stay-at-home dad. The memories. That's your paycheck. That's the investment in the memory bank that you will go back to over and over again.

Maybe you truly could do all of this without leaving the house. If so, hats off to you. But there is a world of memories out there. You just have to go and make them happen. At the very least, your kids need some interaction. One of the final humps that I had to overcome was the realization that if I didn't have friends, then neither did my kids. The isolation is that strong. I realized that I couldn't be my kids' entire world.

However, the world is scary as fuck. What happens if I forget a diaper and the kid has a blowout? Or even worse, if the car breaks down on the side of the highway? All of that is intimidating.

Well, let's get straight to the climax then and stop the worrying. All that shit is going to happen. Yup, you are going to have magnificent fuckups and they are going to be glorious. They are going to be your family stories that the kids will tell over and over again. These are the memories that will fuel you through the grind and the hard times.

But you're going to make it through every single one of those disasters with a smile on your face because I'm going to teach you how. Take solace in the fact that your screwups are in no way going to top mine. I'm so good at this because I've been so very, very bad at this.

You like lists by now, right? Okay, here is the father of all lists. We almost pantsed a Mormon tour guide. I've run into the women's restroom no less than three times in three different locations. My daughter's underwear ended up on a tree branch. I took a wrong turn and got stuck in literal cow shit in the middle of nowhere Kansas with no shoes on. I terrified twelve toddlers at a psychiatric museum that was neither fun nor educational. I have been actually swarmed by mosquitos while pushing a stroller through creepy-ass woods with a freaked-out baby. There was an issue with a bat (the bitey kind not the baseball kind; that's a whole separate incident), I accidentally saw a dead body, and I swear to you, Officer, we're just here to hang out and don't want no trouble.

I know what can go wrong because I've been there when it does. But I know what happens when things go right, too.

You like henges? Of course, you do. Who doesn't like henges? I have seen Boathenge, which is different from Woodhenge, which is also different from the two other henges that look exactly like Stonehenge. Truckhenge is in the same place as Boathenge, so that saved time. Yes, I have a thing for henges, just ask the troll that I visited in the sewer grate next to a river, which I am not making up at all. He's really there in Wichita, Kansas, on the way to a henge.

My point is that there is a world to discover, and all it takes is a single step outside your door once you find your confidence. When you do, you'll have the stories of a lifetime filled with colorful characters.

It just takes a little bit of gumption, a whole lot of preparation, and a desire to do things your own way and not the way people think you should do it. So, strap into the car seat. Let's go for an adventure.

## THE BASICS

I do my very best in this book to not be condescending or give you common-sense information for the most part. I try to think back to what I didn't know and hit on those things, or answer the questions that I see come up a ton. I have full faith that you can figure a lot of this out and remember to bring your adventure bag with you.

With all that said, we do have to cover some basics that not every dad may know. Don't worry, we get into the master class stuff later.

### WHAT TO KEEP IN THE CAR

You already know what you need in your adventure bag. This is what you should always carry in your car. Never take these things out, and always replace them as they are used up.

- Extra diapers, butt paste, wipes, a change of clothes.
- Bottle, water, formula.
- Your kid's favorite toy times two in case you lose one out in the world.
- Small first aid kit.
- Airline puke bags, a few extra garbage bags, and Ziplocs. Kids puke all the time.

- Dog-poop bags. Great for a dirty diaper on the road.
- Small tool kit with a knife, pliers, and duct tape for quickly repairing whatever breaks.
- Assorted bungee cords of different lengths. Always handy to have, from wrapping up a sleeping bag to tying a favorite toy to the stroller.

## FROM THE DADS GROUP

**MICK:** Always have a towel in the back somewhere for when the kids get wet and you want to protect your car seats. It's also great for cleaning up unexpected spills.

**LARRY:** If you are still changing diapers, keep a very small toy that you only bring out during a difficult change. It's a great distraction and will make things go quicker.

**JAKE:** If you have kids with long hair, always keep a hairbrush and extra hair ties in the minivan. You go through both very quickly.

**MIKE:** Don't overload your adventure bag. Just grab what you need from your car and go. Your back will thank you later.

## KID-SAFE PLACES

There are plenty of places that are made for the kids and you. These are the activities and places that are easy to find and often advertised everywhere. Most likely, it will be very stress-free, which is awesome for first timers. Many of these activities are close to your home and, for us, are the perfect starter adventures until you get your sea legs.

Be prepared to be the only dad there. Own it. There may be times when no one is going to sit next to you at story time. It's cool, I get it. Sometimes my handsomeness is intimidating.

If you do see another dad out at the park or story time, give him the required head nod. This acknowledgment is steeped in tradition, originally started in 1245 when Sir Killington gave a head nod to the French at the Battle of Bordeaux Wine Box. It's a sign of respect, and the fact that both of you are out there demands a certain level of decorum.

Now, onto the adventures. Start with your local library and make friends with the head librarian. I believe that this is the twelfth time I've mentioned this, so by now your kids should be calling her Auntie. Libraries hold more than just story times. They have a ton of programs for young ones, both in school and out. Even if your child isn't walking yet, get them there and sit on the floor. Sing songs, hokey pokey your butt off, and give homage to the itsy-bitsy spider on its impossible climb to the water spout. Normally, there is a calendar of events that you can find on your library's website. These include kid sing-alongs, puppet shows, or sometimes even Excel for Toddlers. I made that last one up, but it would be funny. The point is, the library is your hub and there are tons of parent-child activities.

Let's move on to parks. Easy enough. Nothing beats a picnic at the park. It is the dream. Sunshine and grass. Slides and ladders. Sandpits and our hatred for them. A heads-up, though, this is where some guys do get confronted by moms groups. I know enough guys who this has happened to that it's more than myth. Every once in a blue moon a very pesky know-it-all seems to want you to "prove" that you have a kid at the park. I think they probably have been watching too much evening news. If it does happen, smile and point out your kids.

Bounce houses and play places are springing up everywhere, and these are pretty great. There is usually plenty of seating if you can't fit your butt through the rope maze. But be prepared, because if you are a dad, you will be mobbed by children in a good way. There is nothing more fun than a dad in the climbing equipment playing tag. This is your rock star life, enjoy it!

Community centers are also great places to go that very much have families in mind, especially when it's cold out. There may be some sort of membership fee, but in my experience, they are worth it. There is one here with an open gym for toddlers every Friday that costs a buck a kid. I've spent hours at this place with my dads group. There are also pools and tracks, and other events are held there. Get on their mailing list.

Zoos and science museums are always a family favorite. They are relatively easy. Look into season passes if at all possible. These are great things to visit when you have nothing to do. I've had a season pass to my zoo for nine years. I've got a system down. I can do half the zoo in three hours, have a picnic lunch, and be back in time for naps. At this point, I can give personalized tours of the zoo, including all the cool secret zoo stuff. There is a bird show at ten and two. Science museums are great for winter, but be careful with the immersive movies they show at places like this. They are fun, if your kid can handle it. That's on your shoulders, but look into a season pass there as well. No matter what ages your children are, there is plenty at both the zoo and the museums to entertain your child and you.

## DAD HACK

In the spring, don't go to the zoo or the science museum on Fridays. Those are days that school field trips usually show up at the end of the year and it can get very crowded. Instead, show up on a Tuesday morning when it opens and have the whole place to yourself.

Then there are the Mommy and Me classes. Some of these are done by private organizations but others may be offered by your city. Check out the city's parks and rec website. City-sponsored activities are often cheaper than those offered by private companies, but both are easy. I took a horse-riding class with my daughter when she was four. I didn't ride any horses, mainly because they are huge and I'm pretty sure they want to eat me. Don't let the Mommy and Me tag intimidate you either.

Also, start following local mom and dad bloggers, parents' magazines, and your city's tourism website. All these are great for finding adventures and events that you are not aware of. They are all also the best places to find coupons and free-admission tickets. I would sometimes schedule my week based on what coupons I had available. This comes out more in the budget chapter, but I mention it here so you can keep your eyes open.

Finally, get to know the parents around you, whether they are your neighbors or people from church or the liquor store. More experienced parents will know the inner workings of a lot of places. This list is not exhaustive because it can't be. There are always things popping up. I personally like festivals that start on Thursdays because everyone else is at work. It's almost like we have the whole renaissance fair to ourselves.

This is a good starter pack for you to work on. It's designed to get your confidence up because there is so much more out there that you are not really aware of yet.

Whether you live in a city, suburb, or rural area, there are things around you that are made for kids. It can take some time to find them, but don't count anything off the list until you try it. Some adventures will be great, and like I've said, some will fail wonderfully.

Now, what about the mall playground?

Look, mall playgrounds are where dads go so their souls can die. They are germ-infested little petri dishes that grow Ebola. Every time a dad walks into a mall playground, his sperm count goes down. It's a scientific fact that I just made up. Take the risk if you want to, but just know that you've been warned. I'm not a fan.

## FROM THE DADS GROUP

**MICK:** Get a portable placemat and keep it with you when you go out on adventures. When you eat out, it just makes things easier because many places that we end up going aren't the cleanest.

**LARRY:** There are so many germs and snot on everything when you go out. Take disinfecting wipes with you.

> **JAKE:** You're not going to go out every day, of course. The house still needs to be clean. But always have two or three options nearby that are easy if the kids need to burn off energy. It will make the rest of your day easier.
>
> **MIKE:** When money is tight, or you just don't have a lot of time, the mall playground is worth it. So, it's a last resort kind of thing, but sometimes your hands are tied.

# DAD UP THE ADVENTURES

You are ready for the next step in adventuring with your kids.

You need to fundamentally change your thinking, but by this point that should be second nature. Do you really want to go to the sing-along every Friday at ten? Is sitting by yourself at story time just not cutting it anymore? Has boredom sapped your will to change diapers?

Eventually, you will come to the same truth that we experienced at-home dads have figured out: the kids don't really care where they go as long as they are with you.

That's it. That's the secret. It's not so much where you go that is the attraction. It's you they want to spend time with. You're an amusement park rolled up into a security guard with bulging biceps and a utility bag. I was going to say you're just like Batman and then realized that in this case it's a really bad analogy. Don't be Batman.

First off, don't limit yourself to the ordinary. That sucks. Think about the word "anything." If you could do anything with your time with the kids, what would you do? Don't think about what would make the kids happy. Think about what would make YOU happy.

You know what a Civil War battlefield is? A giant field. Do you know who loves to run in giant fields? Your kids. Do you see where I'm going with this?

Don't let art museums freak you out. There are often children's programs there where the kids get hands-on experience. Yes, everything is priceless, but on the flip side if they broke a five-dollar bowl at a store, you couldn't afford that either. There are ways to be careful and have a good time.

My kids do not play baseball, but they loved the Negro Leagues Baseball Museum. I loved the history. We ran bases and talked about Satchel Paige. Then we went to the historic home of Alexander Majors, the founder of the pony express. Who loves ponies? Kids. Who loves pony express mail? Me.

The great thing about a lot of these museums is that younger kids often get in free or for very low cost. Once you open yourself to things that are not normal for kids (because someone decided that?), then the whole at-home dad experience changes. Yes, let's acknowledge that it is a bit stressful trying to keep a two-year-old off the priceless chair, but that counts as a workout. And believe me, once you do this enough, they get the hang of it. If there is any museum around you, it is worth checking out. Here in my neck of the woods, I've seen everything from the Airline History Museum to Leila's Hair Museum, which I have been to on three separate occasions (and it's not as creepy as you would expect).

Okay, we've got all the museums covered, but that's just the start. Go deeper. What else is out there? What might be unusual?

A tour of the grocery store. Didn't see that coming, did you? After all, you are at the store three times a week. But that's different from a tour. Mick set this one up for us. Get your dads together and talk to the manager. Most likely, the manager will love to give you a behind-the-scenes tour of the bakery, seafood, or produce department. Then go further and look at the businesses around you. What would be good to see? The craft coffee factory? Yup, we had a nice French press there, although the kids did not enjoy the actual taste. Then the motor home factory, which was awesome. What about the craft brewery? Can you even take kids to those? Sometimes, although usually it's a bad idea to let them into the tasting.

You're feeling apprehensive about all this. I can tell. I can hear you suck in your breath as you turn the pages. You're thinking, *But what will people think if I take them to a bar?* Tell your great-aunt Bess to go clutch her pearls somewhere else. Get out in the world.

History has always been big for me, so I search out as much historical stuff as I can. I want the experience, and I want the story. You know who tells a great story? Dead people. Graveyards are a magnificent adventure. There are so many historic graveyards around the country that you practically trip on them. And grave rubbings are an amazing craft activity. Just make sure you adhere to any rules posted and be gentle, especially with any older stones.

I've got the rubbings from the tombstone of Jesse James in my office, right next to Bloody Bill Anderson's and the Younger brothers'. Vivi accidently ate grave dirt, which worried me, but she appears okay now.

And always talk to the people who run these sites. Talking to people who have a passion is amazing. I don't care what it is, find that person and you'll always have a great time. You will be surprised what can happen when you ask someone what they are into.

Let's go back to Boathenge. The guy who ran it was a blast. Apparently, he got pissed at his county because they said he couldn't have old boats on his property unsecured because it was also in a flood zone. So, he dug a hole for each one and concreated a boat in there. As we toured his wonderful weirdo world, a fucking peacock jumped on top of an old trailer. I have no idea where he got a peacock from, but it was awesome. Here's to you, Mr. Topeka Boathenge Peacock man. I love you.

The kids expect to see these things with me now, and sometimes they search them out on their own. They will come to me and say, "Dad, there is a giant typewriter. Can we go see it?" You're damn right we can.

You never know what you'll find. Sometimes it's a peacock following you around a bunch of boats, and sometimes you accidently walk into a quilting circle and you get a lesson on how that works. The quilting circle ladies are very, very nice.

## What the Dads Do

*Whenever my kids do something "athletic," like running full speed and launching themselves into the couch, I interview them the way NBA or NFL announcers talk to players after a game, as in, "Jake, tell the folks back home what you were thinking when you completely sacrificed your body right there?"*

**Jared Bilski, father of two**

*Geocaching. It's a great way to get outdoors with the kids no matter what age they are and it's a ton of fun.*

**Danny Adams, father of nine**

*Bubbles. So many bubbles. Both a blessing and a curse.*

**Grady Black, father of one**

*Art museums. At the end of the visit, find a nice spot away from everything valuable and have the kids draw what they have seen. Bring your own supplies!*

**Randy Holt, father of two**

*We build electronic projects, which includes soldering, mechanical assembly, and coding. Bike rides and board games. D&D and tons of reading. We make butterbeer and blue bantha milk and ice cream. We practice* Fortnite *emotes and built the ISS in* Minecraft. *You never know what your child will be interested in but be patient and keep presenting them with opportunities.*

**Ed Johnson, father of two**

*Camping! At night, take the kids for a walk around the tent so they can see there is nothing out there. This makes getting them to bed easier.*

**Paul Bartlett, father of two**

*I pile all the stuffed animals into the car and tell my son we are taking them on a tour of the town.*

**Jordan Sass, father of one**

*Estate sales are a great place to take the kids and have a little bit of fun, save a little money, and keep Dad interested!*

**Jonathon Abbot, father of three**

*Driveway Olympics. I keep assorted balls, bats, and gear in my garage for those days we just need to get active. Games like four square or kickball. Or better yet, Calvin Ball, a game where the rules are made up and there are no rules!*

**Micah Maciejewski, father of three**

*We started a family video game night. The games change over time, but the kids look forward to it and it's a great way to bond. Everyone loves it.*

**Damien Michael, father of five**

*We do a lot of demo work and home improvement together. My wife is a solid carpenter, too. My oldest learned how to run new electrical circuits, and my middle son turned an old tool shed into a middle school hangout. Part of the fun is learning with them as we go!*

**Adam Nafziger, father of three**

*When my wife is working from home, we go streaking through the bedroom while she is on a work call. Everyone has a great laugh!*

**Billy Doidge Kilgore, father of two**

*My three-year-old daughter is helping me make ax-throwing targets. She isn't too bad with a drill.*

**Aaron Smith, father of one**

*It doesn't matter if you can carry or tune or not, singing! From Raffi to Metallica, I've always loved singing to my kids when they were babies. They just wanted to hear my voice and it calms them down.*

**Aaron Yavelberg, father of two**

*We make kites and fly them together! We used old onesies and leftover fabric, twine, and a package of dowel rods. If you want your kite to be a bit more stable, make sure there are a few hole slits for the air to pass through.*

**Stephen Herman, father of two**

*My son is five months old, so mostly we just fart together.*

**Seth Staples, father of one**

## FROM THE DADS GROUP

**MICK:** You have to look out for poison ivy. If you're out in nature, always be aware of where the kids are walking. Kids love to roll around in grass and walk off trails, and that stuff can make a good day turn into a bad week.*

**LARRY:** State parks usually have great one-of-a-kind adventures and are very cheap. Always bring plenty of water, sunscreen, extra clothes, Band-Aids, and bug spray. If you're camping, that list gets a lot longer.

**JAKE:** Be active and go do stuff even if it seems lame. You never know when you are going to have a thing happen that you talk about for years. We once went to what Shannon called a "waterfall" together as a group. It was the smallest thing and was really more field runoff. I climbed up to get a picture and fell on my butt. I smashed my phone and my foot landed in the poop water. But it's a memory that we still joke about. Also, don't climb stuff in flip-flops.

**MIKE:** Race day at the speedway is the best. It's not usually crowded on practice days and is either very cheap or free. You can bring in your own snacks, which

---

* Author's note: Mick has some serious personal issues with poison ivy. I think he dreams about it. Follow him around for a day, and he'll point out every plant and call it poison ivy. You could be in a parking garage, and he would find poison ivy. He's so obsessed with it that he was demanding an entire chapter just on poison ivy. So there, Mick, I've put poison ivy in the book. Please shut up about it now. But also, poison ivy sucks so follow Mick's advice, but don't let it consume you like it does him.

> saves a lot of money. The kids loved watching the cars and they got excited while I got excited. Just bring plenty of sunscreen, good ear protection, drinks, and comfy shoes.

## HOW TO FIND THE ADVENTURES

"There's nothing out by me," you're saying. My rural dads, come close. Let's chat. You're thinking that I can do all of these things because I live in New York or LA, or at least a large town, right? That's how I'm able to find great adventures. But out by you, no there is nothing but fields. Your town is less than five hundred people and the next big city is two hours away. So no adventures for you, right?

Well, there probably are if you look hard enough. I understand your plight when you live in an area where cows outnumber people. It's even more isolating, and it may feel like the only thing to do is to go to the small library. But I'm going to tell you that there are things out near you that the kids will love. If our Anchorage dads can find adventures, so can you.

I'm not a rural dad, but a good 50 percent of the adventures I have had with the kids were in towns that if you blink, you'll miss. I'm in the suburbs of the Midwest. Across the street I can see a horse and a donkey that we have nicknamed Phineas and Ferb. However, I'm also thirty minutes away from a major downtown. I've certainly done a lot in the cities, but it's the countryside that I really love. Out there, you can find gold.

Rural America is a damn treasure trove of the amazing, and if you're a big-city dad, you need to explore there. I have yet to have a bad meal or service in those small towns that lie between the wheat and corn. There is a ton of shit that is unique to the countryside and that you can't find anywhere else. The World's Largest Rifle? Middle of Iowa. Twenty-foot dive into a quarry? Missouri. Ax throwing for kids? Oklahoma. There's a missile silo in South Dakota and a piece of the movie set from *The Flintstones* in Arkansas. Those two aren't related, although one bombed bigger than the other.

So let's talk about how to find everything. When people hear about what I've done, this is what they want to know: How do you find all of these things?

Well, for starters, get three different lists going.

1. Activities in my town
2. Day trips
3. Overnights

Next comes the research phase. Write down all you know in whichever list it applies. It took me ten years to see everything on my list within an hour of my house. All the museums, attractions, and oddities, but I did it.

Let's start with websites. There are two you need to become familiar with: Roadside America and Atlas Obscura. Roadside America breaks down the entire US by state and is populated by people like me and you. Visit one of the maps and start clicking around and seeing what's near you. For example, in Haydenville, Ohio, population 419, there is a round house that looks interesting. Which is good because it's not far from the World's Largest Washboard and a festival in Logan, Ohio. That actually sounds awesome. I've taken the kids to an occult museum, but not a giant washboard. I bet there is some jug music, and what kid doesn't like jug music? And while we are in Logan, we can stop by the pencil sharpener museum. I had no idea that was even a thing, but that seems like something I want to do.

See, that took ten minutes. Actually, if you're in Ohio, there's a year's worth of shit up that way. Cool. I'm going to Ohio soon.

Next up: Atlas Obscura. I love this one as it breaks down each state and has longer write-ups of what's there. It bills itself as "the definitive guide to the world's hidden wonders." That's what you want.

So, let's do New Mexico. I've never been. A quick search of Atlas Obscura lets me know about the Musical Highway, which looks bitchin'. Then, of course, Roswell and the International UFO Museum and Research Center. But we're not done, not by a mile. The Bitsi Badlands in Farmington, White Sands, and tons of caves.

Not only do these sites give me ideas for trips to take with my kids—because let's be honest, I've got the time—but they also show me things close to or in my own town.

## DAD HACK

Only in Your State is another great website that I've started using. These are articles written by people who live there and give you the insider information and hidden secrets. Sometimes it's self-described tours such as the best doughnut shops in your town or crazy street names that might be good for a short drive when you need to get out of the house.

Next, nearly every city, town, or county has a tourism center. Find the website and check them out. If you have a Twitter account, find them there and reach out to them. This is their job. Ask what's going on, what are the off-the-wall trips, what are the kid-friendly places, and where are the best places to eat.

Also, find the parks and tourism websites of the states near you. Sign up for the newsletters and also their mailing lists. State and national parks are amazing. Request tourist information and most will send you a brochure or magazine. Browse through them to see what might be fun. Apparently, there is an alpaca farm near me that I need to go to. Pay attention to the small advertisements in the back. These are usually mom-and-pop stops that don't have a ton of money to advertise so they keep it tiny. But you'll find some amazing places that way. This is how we found buffalos and fed them corn.

Now, it's time to go more old school. Get off the net and search your public library for books of local history or guides. It's how I found the oldest continuously used church in Kansas. It had been wiped out twice, once by a fire and once by a tornado. But it kept rebuilding, and even had a graveyard dating from the mid-1850s. They were a bit shocked when I showed up on a Friday with a bunch of kids. They were also thrilled to have visitors asking about their history. Then they let the kids ring an actual church bell. That was awesome.

Wherever you are, eat local and talk to people. Servers are the absolute best source of local information in any town. Both libraries and locals provide unique experiences and information. Doing this, you run into accidental adventures. There is an Evel Knievel motorcycle museum in Kansas, which shouldn't be confused with the motorcycle museum in Missouri, which is not far from the

Vacuum Cleaner Museum, which did not suck at all. Talking to a waitress in Colorado, she told me about a road up a mountain that only the locals knew about. My wife wanted to kill me.

Finally, get to know the parents in your town or city. The more experienced ones always have the insider information. You'd be surprised, too, how many actually write about it. Follow their blogs or organizations. There are mommy bloggers everywhere. (Time to catch up, Dads!) There are also smaller parenting magazines and organizations.

And there you go, that's how you find the adventures. No matter if you're in a big city or small town, there are things around you that the kids will love, and so will you.

Just remember, you can do ANYTHING. Take advantage of that. Involve your kids in your interests. Don't limit yourself to the kids-only activities. They want to be with you more than anything. You're their hero.

## WHAT TO DO WHEN THERE ARE NO CHANGING TABLES

You're going to run into situations where there are no changing tables in the men's room. Things are getting better but not good enough that they are everywhere. It's an inconvenience. I mean, what dad never changes a diaper? Are we still like that? What horseshit.

If you run into an establishment that doesn't have a changing table in the men's room, you have some options. You can go the Mike way and learn to change a diaper while you sit on a toilet in the stall. Put the kid on your knees and do some straight-up Cirque du Soleil gymnastics to get the dirty diaper off. On your way out, let the owner of the establishment know that you will be sending him a bill for the Vegas-level show you just put on. And before you ask me, "Why don't you just change the diaper on the floor of the bathroom?" hold your tongue. The minute you go into a men's restroom and lick it is the moment I'll change my kid on the bathroom floor.

Next there is the car seat change, because why the fuck not. I've had to run out of restaurants so I could change a diaper. I love the crowd gathering around me while I try to position my kid in the front seat of my van. In no way do I ever feel like I'll get the cops called on me for being creepy. Which is weird, because from my view, I'm pretty pissed off that I have to show my kids' nether regions to the parking lot attendant in order to change a diaper. You can try changing the diaper by putting the kid in the open trunk as there is usually a lot of space. But if you thought it was a bad look in the front seat, try it with a screaming kid in the trunk.

Jake and Larry have changed diapers in every situation, in every environment. They are magicians that can pull a diaper pad out of thin air and have the kid changed before you even know it happened. It's as if they are able to stop time, and poof, they are done. This has bothered me for many years. They have not told me their secret, but I can only imagine it involves some deal made with otherworldly beings. You will get this fast one day because you have no choice. Wherever you have to do it, it is uncomfortable and awkward when it's in public. If there were a diaper-changing competition, I would 100 percent put my money on Jake or Larry.

Mick's style is my personal favorite, and this is why he is my hero. No changing table in the restaurant? No worries, there's always a booth. He's done it. Mick don't care. If you want to get yourself a nice Google review, then put a changing table in the men's room for God's sake. Your patrons who are eating are going to absolutely love the fragrant smell of baby shit wafting over their chicken chow mien.

This is some bullshit. Moms, help us out here. Dads need to change diapers. We want to be involved. Make a fuss until there is a changing table in every men's room. It's gotta be a thing. I can't see another one of my guys smiling awkwardly when he's just trying to be a good father.

## CRAFT TIME

All of us are going to spend a very large amount of time making things with our children. Whether you're coloring little flowers or getting some glitter work in, craft time with kids is a rite of passage. Besides, you can't adventure every day. Whose budget can take that kind of hit? Not to mention you'd be exhausted. Let's get to crafting like a dad and make some magic snowmen come to life.

The same philosophy that you applied to outside adventures needs to now be applied to your inside adventures. You can do ANYTHING. It's that simple, we just don't think it is because we've spent too much time on Pinterest figuring out how Mom does it.

This is when you get your kids into your hobbies, and it pays off in the long run. If you can vacuum with an infant strapped to your chest, you can brew beer with one.

Whatever your hobby, get your kids into it and then tailor that hobby to fit their abilities. I like to do woodworking, so I

built a ballista with the children. I know you're asking, "What
the hell is a ballista?" For those not up on medieval warfare siege
weapons, it's a giant crossbow. And why did we build it? Because
we had already done a trebuchet and a catapult, so it was the
next logical step in teaching my kids how to storm a castle. And
if we are honest, two catapults turned on their sides is a ballista.
Easy peasy. When it was sunny out, we took a trip to the country
and launched eggs and potatoes. The kids made their own flaming arrows, too. Jake was on standby with a glass of water.

## DAD HACK

The length of the arm of a trebuchet is exactly 1¾ the
length of the base. The height of the trebuchet is the
same as the longest part of the base. For the sling, use
a triangular piece of tough fabric and grommets to at-
tach to the throwing arm of the trebuchet. For the trigger mechanism, use two eyebolts on the frame, and one
eyebolt on the throwing arm. Thread a screwdriver that
is attached to a long piece of rope through these three
eyebolts. Finally, as a safety precaution, no one should
be standing behind the trebuchet. Sometimes it isn't exactly accurate.

I started building things with my kids as soon as they could
walk. I have taken each opportunity to teach them the math, history, and science behind everything we've done. Go ahead and
ask any of them what $a^2 + b^2$ equals. They'll know.

They will also know about the French Revolution because
this past summer we built a guillotine. It was tough to convince
the moms on this one, but I pulled it off with "Nah, it'll be fun.

Don't come home on Tuesday until I tell you, though, okay?" Besides, I didn't actually build the guillotine. The kids did that one all on their own. They built the machine, I just made the blade because that was fucking awesome. Then sixteen kids and I made salad for dinner that night.

This is how you craft like a dad. You do things that you want to do, and you bring your helpers with you. They get screwdrivers, scrap wood, and the bandages when you need them. Don't settle for what you've seen other parents do.

Seek out local woodshops and craftsmen and see if the kids can learn from them. There are amazing places out there that make unbelievable things and are only too happy to show you how it's done or give you a special project for you and your kids. We have been to an 1800s-style woodshop where the kids learned how to use one-hundred-year-old hand tools, including planes and drills. We have also been to an expert who makes hand-crafted kaleidoscopes and he let the kids help.

Build amazing pillow forts complete with couch cushions, teach a two-year-old to roll dice, and you've got yourself an amazing Dungeons & Dragons game. Brew the beer. Bake cookies in the shape of a football team logo. Paint the trebuchet, then burn it in a giant bonfire after the castle has been conquered.

Grab the googly eyes and put them on the milk, the framed family pictures, or the shampoo bottles. Those screams from your wife are really screams of joy after she's done being freaked out. Oh, put the googly eyes on flaming arrows. I'm so going to do that now.

You do you. That's all there is to crafting with kids.

# THE DAYS WHEN YOU DON'T WIN

Not every day is going to be a win. Not every adventure is going to go smoothly. Sometimes, you're going to get your ass kicked.

I know that this chapter is written in the "rah-rah, go get 'em, tiger" attitude, and that is intentional. All the advice is tried and true and really does work. But I only know that it works because I have failed so, so many times.

Let me tell you about the Glore Psychiatric Museum, a museum about the history of a branch of medicine. I didn't do the proper research before going. Turns out, the history of psychiatry is pretty fucked up, and I don't mean in a Scientology way. The museum had mannequins being burned at the stake, shut up in little wooden boxes, or just flat-out electrocuted. I brought five dads and twelve kids under five to that nightmare.

All the mannequins happened to look like Mom.

The kids freaked out. At one point, Luke (Larry's kid) and Vivi jumped a velvet rope to save the poor mom who was about to be dunked in a giant vat of fake water. There was screaming and crying, and that was just Jake. It was brutal. It was like running a marathon from one disaster to the next. But to the kids' credit, if they had a crowbar, they would have freed a lot of mannequin moms that day.

"Excuse me," a docent said.

"I'm trying!" I screamed back at no one in particular. "Where's Wyatt? Wyatt, get out of that shock therapy chair! That is not a toy!"

You want to talk about parental judgment, well, there it is. This one was all on me. It went south so fast. At one point, Vivi and Adam (Larry's older kid) joined hands and huddled together as we tried to push through the museum and to the glorious exit. I've had better days. I don't even want to talk about the gift shop.

Some adventures and crafting are going to turn out that way. Once, I was building with Wyatt when he was three. I asked him to hold my hammer. He smashed the hood of my car.

You need to know what to do when things go bad. It's for those days when you just don't have it, don't want to leave the bed, and can't afford car repairs. Believe me, my dads and I have messed up so many times, so take our knowledge from ten years of chaos. Also, my apologies to the Cornhuskers.

- **Always have a backup.** When the place you go to isn't going to work out, or it's closed, or it costs too much, have something in your back pocket.
- **It's okay to cut bait and run.** No shame in the dad world.
- **Learn to say "I'm sorry" with the most sincerity you can muster.** The sad truth is, dads have a really low bar for success. It's bullshit, but it's true. When you mess up, give an *I'm sorry* and most people will be cool with that.
- **Have AAA or some other car service on speed dial.** Car troubles are one of my big fears. This helps manage that fear.
- **Be easy on yourself.** You can't be super every day. Every hero needs some downtime.
- **Go with the flow.** It's in the struggles where we learn. Remember that when it gets bad.
- **Learn new hobbies.** Not every hobby is going to be great to do with kids, so find the ones that are and get into them a little bit.

- **Make notes of your stopping point in museums.** When you inevitably have to leave early, remember the last museum placard you read. That way, when you come back, because you will, just start wherever you left off.
- **Take pre-walkers to museums.** Before your kid learns to walk is the absolute best time to go to a museum.
- **Pack a lunch or snacks for the kids.** A hungry kid is a cranky kid.
- **Create a car entertainment box.** Place a box of coloring books and crayons in the car. When the kids are bored, this keeps them entertained.
- **Play zone defense.** When in a group, employ the zone defense. For example, Larry's by the swings, I've got the sandpit, Mick handles the slides. Group parenting rocks.
- **Order meals through Dad.** Too many voices make servers pissed. Dad orders everything.
- **Chicks dig scars.** No explanation needed.
- **Read the ENTIRE website of wherever you are going!** I should take my own advice.

You're not going to adventure every day. You're not going to craft. That shit would get absolutely exhausting. Some days are built for staying home and letting the kids be kids inside. Embrace those days as well and recharge your batteries. And please don't feel like you need to do any of the things I've mentioned. Remember, I've been at this a long time and that's a lot of days to fill.

More than anything, though, have faith in yourself. You've got this.

## ≡ *Because Dad Says So . . .*

*Unless your kid is 100 percent potty trained, put them in Pull-Ups when you travel long distances. You can still take them potty when you stop, but you never know when you're going to get stuck in traffic, on a runway, waiting for a cab, or they might fall asleep. I learned this the hard way.*

**Joe Auger, father of three**

## FROM THE DADS GROUP

**MICK:** When it's been a disaster, still try to end the trip on a positive note. That will put you and them in a better mood for the rest of the day. Don't be afraid to get up and try it again the next day.

**LARRY:** Expect things to go wrong. Things are not going to be perfect. It's how you respond to it that is going to change the situation.

**JAKE:** You have to roll with it when shit goes wrong. Have a plan in place but adjust it as needed.

**MIKE:** Don't be afraid to lean on the other dads when it's not your day. Let them know that it's not working and ask for help.

# CHAPTER 6

# BUDGETS, SIDE HUSTLES, AND GOING BACK TO WORK

The person who said money can't buy happiness probably had a lot of money.

## WORDS OF WISDOM

Know that going in you are going to have to make sacrifices. But also know that you didn't choose to be a stay-at-home dad alone. Share the load of budget pressure and communicate with your spouse to get on the same page. You both valued having someone at home. It's not easy, but having the right motivation in the beginning really helps. This is a choice that you made together. Be mindful, be present, and really enjoy the time you have with the kids. It goes faster than you would think.

*Carl Wilke, father of six*

**T**wo years and eight months into my time as a stay-at-home dad, Erin got fired from her job. It was two months before Christmas. So that sucked.

It's one of those moments that bring all the budget pressures of being a stay-at-home dad right to the front. From relying on someone else to provide for your financial future, to highlighting every bad mistake you've made along the way. None of this is easy, and that constant pressure of money, money, money makes it harder.

And before we get into the rest of this, let me acknowledge a few things here at the beginning. I understand that I am in a privileged position. Erin has done a wonderful job providing for the family day in and day out. We have never missed a bill or house payment in the years that we've done this. That's not to say that we haven't gone through some very lean times, such as when she lost her job three years in, but it also means that I recognize that I am a very lucky bastard.

Erin was able to find a job right before Christmas, but it devastated our meager savings account. I doubt there is a guy reading this book who hasn't dreaded looking at his bank account in the morning on occasion. Some days, I would close my eyes like I was watching a gory scene in a horror movie. Not to mention the complete embarrassment of having your debit card declined at the grocery store. Although, I do appreciate how polite the checkout lady is during those moments.

"There's a problem with the card," she says.

"Oh, well, that is unfortunate," I reply.

"I'm sure it is our system." It's at this point that I really love her professionalism. It's like she is taking one for the team. Perhaps it would have been better if I just gave her an honest answer instead of smiling like an idiot.

"No, I'm broke. I was broke yesterday and I'm going to be broke tomorrow. Let me try an assortment of high-interest credit cards instead to see which one has some room on it. You'll notice when I open my wallet the complete display of how many bad financial decisions I've made. Perhaps we can get together over saltines and discuss my failures in more depth?"

But the story of Erin being laid off—because now I'm being told that she was not fired and I better say it right—is a good way to highlight that huge fear a lot of us have in the beginning. What is our budget going to look like, where can I save money, are there any side hustles, and what do I do about that Grand Canyon–size gap on my résumé?

## WHAT TO EXPECT WHEN YOU'RE EXPECTING MONEY. LET'S TALK ABOUT YOUR BUDGET.

Many at-home dads I've known don't actually talk about budgeting, which is ironically the first step to fucking up a budget. But it's got to get done, so sit down with your significant other and have a serious conversation about money. That's job number one.

I can guarantee you that the dads I've seen who have failed to have this talk with honesty find troubles later down the road. The Talk, with all its implied roadblocks, doesn't have to be hard. Well, yes, it does but I'm trying to ease you into this a bit. It is hard because you and your spouse need to look at exactly what you are spending versus how much money is coming into the house. Then you have to make hard decisions based on your goals. For example, you would like to eat. That's a good goal to have that can be shared by both. Not eating is not a very productive goal.

Luckily, there are plenty of apps and websites out there to help you begin planning a budget, setting goals, and getting on the same page. I would recommend using some budget-tracking software such as Mint or You Need a Budget. Both have the tools to find out exactly what you are spending and where it is going. There are plenty of systems and philosophies to browse through as well. Look them up, together, and start making some decisions.

Take the time to listen to your spouse's concerns and questions as well as voicing your own. If that is your starting point, now we can get into how things are going to change for the at-home parent. Just keep in mind I'm in no way a financial guru or expert, I've just fucked up a lot.

"How?" you may ask. I was once building Vivi a dollhouse because I could do it for fifty bucks and make it better than the $200 models that she really wanted. I went to the craft store for some decorations for the little rooms. One thing led to another and I walked out of there after spending $230. First off, that dollhouse was bitchin' and got passed around the dads group for years. And second, Erin and I had a huge fight about my fuckup and then I begged her to return a lot of it because I couldn't face the shame. This is just one of the many, many, many mistakes I've made with budgeting.

Also make sure you talk about personal money with your significant other. I've heard some guys getting "allowances" from their wives. I've talked this over with my dads and we have come to this conclusion: fuck that shit. I'm going to give a shout-out to the moms here on this one. There have been studies on how much

## DAD HACK

Pay bills together and make a night of it. This not only allows both you and your significant other to be involved in the decision-making process, but it also spreads out the budget pressure that comes from that. One of the biggest mistakes I made was paying bills by myself for years. Now we do it together and make a date night out of it.

what we do is worth, and no one can afford us. The idea that I would get an "allowance" when I'm busting my ass and sacrificing for the family is some bullshit. Moms, if your significant other gives you the "allowance," I got your back. That is insane and is going to create problems down the road. I'm not a paid servant, and you can stick your allowances up your ass. Sorry, this one makes me mad.

My wife and I consider the money she makes to be our money. We both made sacrifices to have someone stay home with the kids. We both work for a living, just in different fields. And believe me, my ass will go on strike. The honest truth is that if the income my wife makes wasn't considered ours, I would walk away from being an at-home dad.

My best advice is to really sit down with your spouse and find out what your recurring bills are. And please keep in mind that both your voice and your wife's voice are important here. You each need to be heard. If one side feels like they are being brushed off, it's going to lead to a lot of fights down the road. And there's a natural power play during some of these conversations that I've seen. "Well, I make all the money, so I make all the decisions." That's not how this shit works. That's going to build resentment.

Do yourself a favor and revisit this talk every six months to evaluate your progress.

## THINGS TO CONSIDER

Some bills will be lower. For example, your clothing budget is going to go down for you. That's nice, right? You can wear jeans until they are barely hanging on. You're not trying to impress anyone anyway. This is basically Mick's philosophy. Also, he is a cheap bastard.

You can expect your utility bills to go up, which caught me off guard. But with you home, that means more electricity, water for laundry, and gas for the heater.

Gasoline is a fickle one and depends completely on you and your location. For me, I budget twenty-five dollars a week on gas. When that runs out, I stop going out. It's limiting but it does help me plan my week. For trips that I know are going to be longer, I put it as a line item in the budget. Some trips have taken me months to save up for.

Your food bill is the most inconsistent bill you'll have and is hard to really pin down. Not only does this fluctuate depending on region and family, but there is also a big quality issue. Eating healthier is typically more expensive.

There are also unknown expenses when it comes to kids. They are small things that pop up out of nowhere, and they hit both the food budget and other areas. My experience has taught me that I will never have all the ingredients I need for the week or I will run out, even if I thoroughly plan my meals, which I do.

And obviously, your childcare expenses are going to go way down. For my wife and me, this was the number-one deciding factor in whether I should become a stay-at-home dad or not. We all know how outrageously expensive childcare is, and once we ran the numbers, it looked like the only reason one of us was working was for someone else to take care of our kids. That was twelve years ago, and it's only gone up from there.

## DAD HACK

A daily scrum has worked well for my wife and me when it comes to maintaining our budgeting. We both sit down in the morning and go over our accounts. It gets us on the same page, and we review what we've spent and are able to think about any upcoming expenses that may be out of budget. It takes less than five minutes and is a good way to start our day.

## STRETCHING A PAYCHECK

A quick search online for "frugal living" will yield enough results that you could print them all off and comfortably wallpaper your kitchen. Try it and you are already living frugally, except printer ink would put you in the poorhouse. So handwrite them on old grocery sacks. Now you're really living that frugal lifestyle! Parents take frugal living to extreme limits. You don't have to, of course, unless you like Google search results as your decor. Just don't use the ones from your browser history.

The level you take this to is entirely up to you, and cutting spending does not mean living without fun. It just means that if you were rich, you would have way more fun. For the rest of us, what it really means to stretch a paycheck is to spend each dollar with intention. Know where your money is going, what you can do without, and what you are overpaying for.

There is a lot of information available on how to cut spending, from your local library to entire online communities devoted to saving and to getting out of debt. Just keep in mind that what may work for one may not work for another, depending on where you live, your age and income, and your doughnut-supply needs.

I would also recommend checking out podcasts on this subject. There are some great ones out there that take things step by step. My personal favorites are *2 Frugal Dudes* and also the *Frugal Friends Podcast*. They approach frugality as saving money, not as a way to prevent you from having fun. Both podcasts have a large number of back episodes on a range of topics, from saving on trips and paying down debt to spending each dollar with intention.

Here are some highlights that can help you cut spending. This list isn't exhaustive by any means but serves as your jump start to learning how to stretch your paycheck.

## Because Dad Says So . . .

*If you have the room, a stand-alone freezer is great. You can buy in bulk, which is going to save you money. However, when you do buy in bulk, don't buy perishable items. You'll never finish them before they go bad and you'll have to throw them out. Bread is a great bulk buy that freezes easily and defrosts quick.*

**Vernon Gibbs II, father of three**

GROCERIES: Your grocery bill is one of your most flexible. Needs and prices fluctuate weekly. Coupons come into play here as well. But in general, try the following: Plan your meals out weekly, limit your trips to the store, buy what's on sale, buy items that give you a discount on other items, and make dinners from scratch, which can be very fun. Box leftovers for lunch the next day. Farmers' markets are wonderful for saving a few bucks. Shop at a variety of grocery stores to get the best deals. Also, look into grocery store cash-back apps that give you small amounts of money for buying featured products. Do that throughout the year and you can handle some Christmas presents by the end. Invest in a deep freezer and a vacuum sealer. Buy in bulk when possible and if you can afford the initial hit to the budget. If you want a new hobby, try canning. Mick and Larry both do this, and we enjoy some great salsa throughout the year. Although, if I'm honest, Mick's pickled green beans are pretty awful. Sorry, Mick, I really tried to like them. If you have a green thumb, growing your own herbs is a huge money saver because some of that shit is fucking expensive.

Growing a bigger garden is a great idea that a lot of dads do. I pick Mick's garden when he's out of town and when he doesn't know about it.

### Because Dad Says So . . .

*Place a tip jar in the middle of the dinner table, make a little extra cash from little patrons.*

**John Abbruscato, father of two**

**LOYALTY CARDS:** A great way to save some money and get some deals is to join the loyalty programs of many stores and businesses. My biggest accomplishment happened this week. I spent .009 cents per gallon of gas using my grocery store loyalty card. You read that right, less than a cent for a gallon of gas. I took a picture and sent it to my wife in the middle of the workday. Many businesses, such as Target, will also offer you rewards for shopping through their apps. But keep in mind that it's your information they are after and make your own call. For me, it was worth receiving junk mail. I mean, eleven cents! I can use the junk mail to start my grill.

**HOME REPAIRS:** You can teach yourself to do a lot of the house repairs and save the cost of expensive specialists. If your toaster is busted, someone has made a video on how to repair it. I replaced the drum belt on my dryer. It took me all day, but I saved the cost of a new dryer or a repairman. Jake helped me replace my water heater when it busted. John from the dads group helped me replace the blower on my furnace. The five dads redid both Jake's bathroom and kitchen all the way down to the studs. For building repairs and remodels, look for discounted materials. Scratch-and-dent stores are a great way to replace appliances. Let's be honest, kids are going to kick that shit anyway. Habitat for Humanity has stores in many areas that resell construction materials such as toilets, tile, and paint that weren't used on a project. You get a deal; they get to fund the next home. That is awesome.

UTILITY BILLS: Remember your dad always freaking out about the thermostat? This is fucking why. Now that you are on the other side of it, you finally get it! Shut the damn door. Utility bills take up a huge chunk of the budget. Look into programmable and digital thermostats. Keep up to date on replacing your air filter so your HVAC doesn't have to work too hard. Also, look into getting energy-efficient light bulbs, installing window coverings to keep out heat or cold, and unplugging unused electronics. Look into using dryer balls to cut up to 25 percent off your dryer time. Also, a clothesline isn't just for Grandma anymore. Finally, check your toilets and make sure they are low flow and the flapper on the back sits snug. It's an easy fix that will stop costly leaks over time. Invest in some water-saving showerheads, and always check your weather stripping around doors and windows.

CLOTHING: Know where all your thrift stores are and make them the first place you shop for you and the kids. Gently used clothes have saved us hundreds. I'm wearing my pants from one now. Not underwear, though. There are only so many sacrifices I'm willing to make. For children's clothes, there are tons of resale shops and consignment sales that you can find on websites like Just Between Friends. Don't discount garage sales. In the summer until the kids were five, all their play clothes came from a weekend of garage sales. Mike has a nose for these things. Apps such as Yard Sale Treasure Map and Garage Sale Map have been great with getting all the sales in my area together. I can usually set alerts as well. Fifty cents for a shirt and a buck for pants. After twenty bucks, my kids were ready to go, and if the clothes got ruined, I didn't have to worry about it. There are also tons of online marketplaces to check out.

ADVENTURES WITH KIDS: Look for museums that let kids in free. Many don't charge until the age of five. Also, pack a lunch and skip the restaurant. If you do go to a restaurant, try splitting a kids' meal between children, as many don't finish their servings anyway. Some museums offer lower prices during the week and in the morning. If you can't get free admission, attempt to find "buy one, get one" admission tickets. Also, talk to your local tourism board. They may give you free tickets in exchange for a write-up of the activity. I wrote for our local tourism website in exchange for tickets and tours. Finally, visit mom blogs and web pages to see if they are offering any coupon codes. If you're going with your dads, see if you can get a group rate.

This list isn't meant to be exhaustive. Frugality is one of those things that you can take as far as you want.

I didn't mention a specific way to save big money, because honestly, I don't know if you are ready for it. Grocery store coupons. I'm not talking about shopping with an appropriate number of coupons and making friends with your checkout person. (Hi, Linda!) I'm talking about Extreme Couponers. They make frugal people look reasonable.

## EXTREME COUPONERS

In a moment that will forever stand out in my mind, on a warm summer Monday morning, I headed to the local big-box store. I needed some shoelaces and a gallon of milk, for unrelated reasons. Near the checkout, I picked up a candy bar, because I deserve chocolate sometimes.

As I walked toward the checkout line dreaming of my new

shoelaces enjoyed over a glass of milk, feral movement caught my eye. A male and a female, wild haired and frothy mouthed, raced to the lone checkout lane. Three carts' worth of crap pulled behind them like a demented train. I swear a wolf howled in the background. This was my first interaction with what we all now call Extreme Couponers.

Let us define some terms. A person who uses coupons is what we call Normal in the stay-at-home dad world. You often see these Normal people walking around your grocery store smelling like a combination of freshly baked cookies and free samples of laundry detergent.

An Extreme Couponer, however, is much different from a Normie. An Extreme Couponer may masquerade as a frugal individual, but this is merely a cover. What they really want is to see the world burn.

An Extreme Couponer works by stacking coupons on top of coupons and then combining them with in-store specials. It is rumored that many chemical weapons scientists from 1918 began as Extreme Couponers.

Armed with their three-ring binders full of coupons and contracts with the devil, they head to the store to destroy your well-maintained schedule. Your best bet is to run when you see them. The slightest eye contact will signal a challenge where they will yell, "Do you have any coupons? Where are your coupons? Hand over your coupons or face my wrath!" It's very dramatic.

These two particular Extreme Couponers quickly cut me and my shoelaces off at the pass and barricaded themselves in with three carts full of crap. It's almost as if they circled the wagons to fend off reasonable behavior. The female smiled at me, her sharpened teeth glistening under the fluorescent light.

"This will only take a minute," the male said, the lie escaping his lips with ease.

One cart contained only shampoo. Another had an assortment of Q-tips, cotton balls, and medical tape. The last cart held their binders full of coupons. I wanted to run, but I couldn't because I had shoelace issues.

*Well, shit balls,* I thought. If I had said that out loud, I would have quickly lost my own shoelace coupon, so I kept quiet for coupon-safety reasons. The checkout girl, no older than seventeen, sprouted a streak of gray hair as the Extreme Couponers loaded their wares onto the conveyor belt.

I'll admit that I didn't truly understand what was happening. Why does one couple need so many bottles of shampoo? Perhaps they run a yak farm, and we all know the importance of a glossy yak coat. I wanted to say something, but it was clear that the bloodlust had already taken them.

What happened next took twelve hours.

The female horsewoman of the coupon apocalypse meticulously removed each corresponding product coupon from her binder as the item was rung up. One by one she proudly, annoyingly, showcased them to the doomed cashier.

"Um, ma'am," the young cashier said. "This coupon is expired." My heart felt pity for the cashier who was about to be devoured.

"Madison, is it?" the Extreme Couponer said.

"It's Rebecca, actually. It's right here on my name tag."

"Madison, you are wrong!"

"About my name?"

"This coupon is still good! It's still good!" Thunder rolled on a cloudless day as the Extreme Couponer spoke.

"It expired last Christmas." That poor, poor girl.

"No, it hasn't!"

"Um, okay," squeaked the checkout girl as tears came to her eyes. The Couponers laughed.

This happened for every coupon. Every. Fucking. Single. One. The Extreme Couponer then tried to combine coupons with the in-house specials. Behind me, a man and woman had time to meet, fall in love, and move to the suburbs. I was the best man at their wedding.

The manager eventually was called in and argued that store policy didn't allow coupons to be used like this.

"Well, that's not my policy!" said the female.

And like a naive idiot, I decided that this was the time to talk.

"You sure do have a lot of shampoo in there," I said. "Yak issues? I get it."

I'm not sure what happened next, but somehow, I lost my shoelace coupon. It's a cloudy memory as I assume my mind is trying to block out the trauma. What I do remember is that by the time the Extreme Couponers were finishing up, I had received my AARP membership card in the mail.

With an Extreme Couponer, it's not about the sale or the savings. It's not about buying necessary things. It's about the hunt, the victory, and the trampling of another person's joy. To them, the exasperated sighs of those behind them are a heavenly chorus.

It is tempting to become an Extreme Couponer. The movement promises savings and opulence. Don't be tempted. You're better than that. Walk away and enjoy life outside of a library's worth of coupons. And if you see an Extreme Couponer out in the wild, beware. Hold your children close and your BOGO hot dog coupon even closer. If they smell your deal, it's over. Your best bet is to play dead until your coupon carcass is picked clean.

Godspeed, everyone. Godspeed.

---

## FROM THE DADS GROUP

**MICK:** See if your grocery store does overlap ads during the week. These are the days where last week's ads meet this week's ads. You can often find some great deals this way.

**LARRY:** When your kid gets into sports, don't be afraid to buy secondhand sporting equipment. Kids grow up so fast that something new is just not worth it. Not to mention if they even want to stay with it.

**JAKE:** Share the car. Take your spouse to work and use that car for everything it's worth. Keep up on the oil changes and the minor upkeep. For repairs, go to the junkyard and grab the replacement parts cheap. Broken door latch? Junkyard that part and install it yourself.

---

## MIKE'S TOP FIVE GARAGE SALE TIPS:

1. Begin to go to the garage sales on Thursdays. Some may not be open, but you get more stuff, less people, and way better selection.

2. Look for preview sales that allow you to come out the night before. It's a great way to find that something specific.

3. Haggle for everything. People are trying to get rid of things and are willing to go lower or combine items.

4. Know your neighborhoods. Learn which neighborhoods are good for what.

5. Find the year-ahead home. These are the homes that have a child just a bit older than yours. So when they have a sale, you can often find clothes that now fit your kids. Remember this house and hit up their sales every spring and fall.

## WELCOME TO THE SIDE HUSTLE

I hate to burst your bubble, but there are no get-rich-quick schemes in existence. Actually, I love bursting this bubble because it's going to save you a shitload of headaches down the road. There are no get-rich-quick schemes, there are just get-less-poor-at-medium-speed schemes. The get-rich-quick "jobs" you see are just a myth that late-night infomercials sell to parents that are too tired to see straight while a newborn screams like she's at a heavy metal concert. Those infomercials are not your friends. They are part of the problem.

You see, out in the world, you as an at-home parent are seen as a big fat bunny. You're very cute with a little button nose and a dollar tucked behind your ear. You are the prey. The infomercial is a hawk that wants to rip your head off. The man with the very bad toupee is telling you how he decided one day to make millions buying and selling real estate and now you can, too!

Models dance around him, and he has a very big bulge in his pants. What you don't realize is that at this point, you are being hunted by a master. It's going to be gruesome.

Welcome to the at-home-parent side hustle. Notice that it's called a side hustle, not a side sit-on-my-ass-and-let-money-be-thrown-at-me hustle. That's a different kind of thing that is usually only legal in Amsterdam and parts of Nevada. The side hustle is honest with you at the very beginning, unlike the fluffy-haired fake-pants-bulge guy on the TV. You have to work for it, and nothing is going to be easy. Sure, dog walking sounds like a wonderful way to make some beer money until the client's dog needs to be walked during nap time. Now it sucks, your client tells other people that you bailed, and you have no more side hustle.

Yes, you can make money at the side hustle as you parent. I have. I was a freelance expert witness for a bit. I got paid to sit in a deposition and have lawyers tell me how wrong I was. Then they yelled at me. No one even offered me lunch. But the joke was on them. My kids yell at me all day and I never get paid for it. Being at a deposition for a lawsuit was like a vacation. I actually used the money I made from that to take my kids on a real vacation, which included being yelled at by toddlers way more vicious than attorneys.

You have to work for this money, the same as any job. You won't get rich fast. There will be no models hanging on your arm. The bulge in your pants is purely genetic. You have to know what you are doing, and this is where I come in. We'll go over common scams like envelope stuffing and bracelet building, show you where the real side-hustle jobs are, and tell you how to work them around a family.

You may come back to me and say, "Shannon, I know a guy who makes $6K a month selling motivational tapes and books over the internet!" I'll say, "Cool, that guy is full of shit and those books are written by people like me, who get paid to write as a side hustle." Also, that dude never paid me because I got scammed as well. I kid, I've never ghostwritten books. However, I have written a lot of radio ads for weed where it's legal. It's a weird niche to be good at, but when you need a weed ad, I'm your guy.

Let's get to it. Step one in the side-hustle business is knowing the scams.

## KNOW THE SCAMS

Let's go back to the furry little bunny that you are. You're very cute just hopping through the forest and having bunny good times. You meet up with the guys and drink some carrot juice, and now it's time to head home. Boom, the hawk tries to gut you. But you're quick. You knew this could happen, which is why you asked your buddy Carl to tag along.

Carl is awesome. He's big, has huge claws, and totally knows the forest. Carl keeps the hawk away because he's a good guy. He says that he will keep walking with you as long as you pay him a monthly protection fee. Sounds good. You pay Carl, and then he ditches your ass in a rattlesnake den. You got scammed by Carl, and as you finally head home, you spot Carl laughing with the hawk right next to your house. Carl is a giant douche canoe.

Scam artists infect the side-hustle world like a staph infection at a back-alley hospital. And irony of ironies, you are their side hustle. The trick to getting back to your burrow in one piece is knowing what to look for and what to avoid. For example, Carl had a bunny-head necklace. You didn't notice because he told good jokes.

So the first piece of advice is to not be stupid. I can't believe I have to say that in this day and age, but there you go. Not you, though; you're not dumb. I'm talking about the other guy. If a deal seems too good to be true, it is. As I've told you, you will not earn a million dollars a week selling pine cones. That's dumb. You can make some extra vacation money by crafting pine cone figurines and selling them online, though. See, that's smart. But honestly, when something comes along, ask yourself if anyone would ever buy the shit they want you to sell. If no, then it's a scam.

Next, never ever use your personal bank account for the side hustle. Nope. Nada. No way. This is how the mystery-shopper scam goes. The scammer tells you to go buy a product and send it to them. They'll send you a check even before you leave and will make that check out for more than the item will cost. You buy the stuff and keep the difference. The problem comes when that check bounces a week later, and you are a grand in the hole. The mystery-shopper gig is bullshit. It doesn't work like that. I'm sure there are some reputable companies that do it, but the fact remains they are hidden in the scam forest. This advice goes for anyone wanting to do money transfers or cashier's checks. It's a scam. So, no bank account. In fact, even for tax purposes, you should have a separate bank account set up to accept side-hustle payments. And ONLY payments for work completed.

Also, beware any bullshit with subscriptions and joining fees. This is how these companies make money off you. YOU ARE THE PRODUCT. Most of these places offer you access to "one-of-a-kind opportunities" or "guaranteed side-hustle listings!" First off, there are plenty of free websites and apps all around. I've joined them and they're fine. This also goes for any "Take our seminars to earn big bucks!" That's Carl in a suit. He's a dick. I'm not saying don't take a class, but go with something with a good reputation. If you want to get a license or improve yourself professionally, then you initiate. If your side hustle requires a seminar, class, subscription, or fee as part of the job, then you are being worked.

I want to touch on commission-based deals as well. These are popping up more and more. I get offered commission deals a couple of times of month. "Hey, I've got a great opportunity for you!" the pitch begins. "Sell four hundred bracelet subscriptions to your friends and family and you will make big bucks! Carl said you would love this!" Commission deals exist, but they are almost always never worth it. The percentage you get is equal to the amount of rainfall in the Sahara. Unless you are with a reputable company or industry, such as real estate or car sales, skip the commission deals. What they really want is to tap into your social network so they can make a quick buck and then move on.

With any job, it's simple. You do a job. You get paid. It's not any more complicated than that. That's why if any company requires you to buy "product" to sell, it's a scam. These are the most popular in the at-home-parent world, and you've seen them a thousand times. Hell, you have friends who do this. It's diet supplements, makeup brands, legging companies that I'm not legally allowed to name. It's knives that cut through tin, magazines that practically sell themselves! It's bullshit. Yes, direct sales are a way to make money, and you can find some reputable places to do it, but mostly they are a waste of time. I have seen people literally destroyed by this.

Example: I investigated elder abuse prior to becoming an at-home dad. Fifteen percent of my investigations were for exploitation of the elderly, where many of my clients would be convinced to buy a ton of lotions and shampoos and then sell them. The problem came when the scammers wanted my clients to buy more and more. They couldn't sell them. But the real rub is when they tried to convince my clients to get their friends to join. I've walked into houses with entire rooms covered in bullshit crap products. It still makes me mad.

If the focus of the pitch is more on recruitment of others, it's a pyramid scheme. It doesn't matter what product they are asking you to sell. Do a quick search for multilevel marketing and you'll see a thousand companies getting sued for this shit. Every time, YOU ARE THE PRODUCT. We've all lost friends to the MLM. They invite you over for what you think is a nice party, and fucking bam, it's a makeup sales pitch, and you know what? They don't even carry my shade of lipstick. First off, passion purple is fucking awesome. Second, I'm never going to talk to you again. And no, I will not send you an affirmation postcard because your "mentor," who looks a fuck ton like Carl, thinks it will motivate you. Eat a dick.

Finally, look out for anything that lacks professionalism. That means poor communication that contains misspelled words, bad grammar, and the phrase *Or Else,* or offices located in eastern Ukraine. Do your research. Especially beware of anyone appealing to your better nature. "I've got sick kids and cancer of the big toe, you surely want to help me out, right? Join now!" Politely spit in their face, let them know it's nothing personal, and then spray yourself down for scam herpes. You are not doing anyone a favor. You are getting paid to work. Period.

Being aware of all this is how you weed out the bullshit opportunities from the good ones. There are a lot of great side hustles out there. You just have to find them. Research the company. Look for online reviews and see what they say, identify the norms in your market, and go into it knowing exactly how you're paid.

Hopefully, you can make it back to your burrow and little bunny family. Just know that Carl is out there recruiting people and they've now got your phone number. Get ready for the robo-calls.

I fucking hate Carl.

## TIME IS A COMMODITY

Everything comes down to time: how much of it do you have, where are you going to sell it, and who's buying. Time is a commodity, no different from corn or soybeans. It's grown by the future and purchased by guys in monocles who cackle when they get their hands on it.

Time is missed dinners, forgotten birthdays, and watching the entire *Human Centipede* trilogy before moving on to the *Sharknado* collection. Time is bad decisions.

> ### Because Dad Says So . . .
>
> *You need to understand what you can reasonably accomplish given your time frames. Make goals that fit that time. I use an app called Strides that helps me focus on the tasks I need to accomplish for that day. It all comes down to how you manage your time.*
>
> **Matthew Buza, father of two**

We are going to start with passive-time gigs that any of us can do. They require very little effort and don't involve the kids at all. They're about making the things you already own work for you. For example, you can rent out anything. Your clothes, your cars or trucks, your trailers, your tools, and your space. For my rural dads, if you have an extra bit of land or a barn, you can open that up for boat storage and undercut marinas. You can also rent out ad space on your car. All are easy to find by doing a quick search on the internet. (Remember to follow the scam guidelines!) There are also apps that connect buyers and sellers for things like this. They are all easy enough to follow, but beware of a couple of things: (1) Know your liabilities. If you are renting out a car, truck, or trailer, make sure you have insurance and know what the driver will cover. (2) Know what will happen if you don't get the rented item back. What are the company guidelines, and how can you be made whole again? As you're browsing through the rental economy, protect yourself first. I know some dads and moms who do Airbnb for their side hustle. There are risks in this, but it remains a pretty solid option.

For my dads who have no time, let's go into you a bit. These are my dads who have babies and toddlers, which makes time go much faster. Everything you can do has to be done with a baby at your side. Being able to complete a side hustle during the day when you are constantly with the kids makes things hard.

It's tough to focus, which is why I don't recommend doing anything that requires concentration. Buying and reselling is a good side hustle for you. My own sister bought baby clothes at garage sales and opened an online store. She made some serious money doing this. The kids were happy to travel all over the city with her. Having your own Etsy store is good side gig if you are a woodworker or a crafter. But the biggest side hustle in the drop-shipping business is Amazon. You buy the products and ship them to the Amazon warehouse. The idea in all of these is to buy low and sell high, which means you've got to constantly be on the lookout for sales and be smart about it. There is money to be made doing all of this, and it really does depend on your schedule and how much time you put into it.

Besides the selling and reselling game, there are a couple other jobs that will help put money in your pocket. Childcare is an obvious one that I've known several guys do. After all, we watch kids all day. A word of warning, though: there are liabilities, and you'll need a license depending on how many kids you have in your home.

There are also companies that pay you to ensure their products are displayed in store properly and then ask you to report back. It's not a huge amount of money, but if you're going to be at a department store anyway, you might as well get paid for it.

### Because Dad Says So . . .

*Having an investment property can be a good way to make a little extra cash, but until you can do it professionally full time, don't look at it as a big source of income. There is some start-up capital you'll need, as well as a repair budget. But if you can do the repairs yourself, it can work. Many times, I have the kids with me when I handle an issue one of my tenants has. Look at it as a long-term investment.*

**Chuck Bennis, father of two**

When you do have small amounts of free time, say during the kid's nap or when they start preschool, you can begin to branch out a bit depending on what you want to do. Content creators thrive in this type of environment. These are my YouTubers, writers, editors, podcasters, and streamers. Monetizing your website or creativity is the dream. But be aware that there is a lot of hustle required for this one. You've got to learn to freelance and to market your services. Without an audience, you won't make any money. Writing can be a little different as there is a submission process, but as with all content creation, it's a very competitive market.

Then there are the service jobs that provide some income. These are for when your kid is in preschool and you've got a few hours a day to get things done. These are your personal shopping gigs for companies like Instacart, not to mention delivering for DoorDash, Postmates, and Uber Eats. There's also housekeeping and pet care like dog walking and pet sitting. For example, Rover is an app strictly for pet care. There are also transcriptionist jobs, but I do want you to beware of these because they are full of Carls looking to fuck you over.

Look for seasonal work such as being a census taker, which is something several dads I know have done. I've also known dads who had a lawn business on the side. There are plenty of apps to connect you to that market. This is a great option for when you only have a couple of hours a day, and it's usually flexible enough to allow you to walk away if something comes up.

Also, look into being a virtual assistant. There are plenty of reputable companies that are easy enough to find and that will hire you out to do odd tasks for individuals throughout your city. This could be picking up dry cleaning to making travel reservations. I've known parents who have used some of their free time to do this.

Finally, we need to talk about nights and weekends, which are the ultimate times for the side hustle for many parents. You can join a number of rideshare companies like Lyft and Uber. This remains a big one in the at-home dad world. The benefits of ride-sharing are that it is flexible and you set your own schedule. The downside is that it's going to take a toll on your car and take real time away from your spouse or kids, who previously bought your time.

Driving for Uber or Lyft, or accompanying seniors to doctors' appointments are all good options. If you are going to do this, though, look into getting a part-time job. Every dads group always has a few dads making a little bit of bank bartending. They are very popular at playgroup. I also know dads who work at hobby shops, retail stores, or lumberyards. When you are using the nights-and-weekends time account, your options open up. This is where many dads, including me, make use of their side hustle.

There are plenty of places to get more advice. Check out side hustlenation.com as well as apps that get really specific. A quick internet search will pull up a lot, and then there are some that do nothing but aggregate all the jobs for you. Just remember, it's all dependent on what kind of time you have. Be realistic and know that when you give it away, you are taking it away from your family. Next, do a bit of research and know what the average pay is for your industry. Content creators, such as my podcasters and bloggers, make less than three dollars an hour, while Uber drivers can make a grand or more a month.

## Because Dad Says So . . .

*I found a nice little side gig knife sharpening. It started out small but it's a good niche to be in. My advice would be to pick something you enjoy doing anyway and see if there is a way to monetize it even just a little bit.*

**Matt Jacobi, father of two**

*I started out playing around with leatherwork and a buddy asked if I could make him something. It wound up being something that several folks liked and then through word of mouth several groups began to contact me. It's really one of those situations where I found a unique product for a unique market.**

**Miguel Gamboa, father of one**

## PROFESSIONAL SIDE HUSTLES

Many dads forget about our old careers when taking on the role of an at-home dad. Remember, you have skills and can put them back to work. This is where I've made the most from my side hustles. They are also the ones that require the most amount of time, have the hardest deadlines, and are the least flexible.

And to be clear from the start, these types of jobs require the absolute most hustle. You've got to learn to market yourself and your services. Having a personal web page advertising your skills is essential and gives you an aura of professionalism.

---

* Author's note: I also know a guy who makes his own chain mail and now I want all three of these guys to get together and make me a bitchin' suit of armor. They could do it.

## Because Dad Says So . . .

*Don't be afraid to reach out to old colleagues. Your name is already known in the field and it makes it easier to find smaller jobs that now fit your schedule. It's more about a personal relationship than anything else. I also used social media to keep up those professional connections. This is how I found one of my side jobs, which was also good for my mental health.*

**Robert Andrews, father of two**

And you're going to have to really network. Your business will grow the most by word of mouth and through the people you know. If there is a meetup in your area of freelancers, engineers, builders, or IT professionals, then go to it. Have business cards printed out.

As you research, remember your time constraints as well versus the amount of money you can make from these jobs. Most likely, many will require you to get a sitter while you finish the tasks. Is the money worth it versus what you've got to pay out? This is a business, so pay attention to your bottom line.

Let's start with some common ones.

### 1. Writers, editors, and creative freelance work.

This seems like the logical place to start as I'm a writer. This goes beyond blog writing. This is freelance work. It's writing ad copy and business posts, and running social media channels. I've known dads who do all of this. Freelancing is competitive as shit and takes some time to get off the ground. You've most likely heard of apps for this, such as Upwork and Fiverr. For the more serious professionals with some experience, Freelancer.com is a good place to start. But in general, it really does come down to networking. With that said, the best thing about this side hustle is its flexibility. Hell, I write a ton while sitting in the bleachers of gyms, in chairs at a soccer practice, or sitting at picnic tables. I also go to freelancer events, network a ton, and have a website, a social media presence, and business cards. My most consistent freelance job is writing satire, which works out well, as dad humor is my niche. Every week I churn out funny articles like "Molotov Cocktails Voted Drink of the Decade." I'm pretty proud of that one.

I want to also talk about sponsorships and brands. Yes, they happen in the blogging world but not as much as you think. I've taken some brand pitches and sold tweets, articles, or posts. The money is not consistent, and I've got to believe in the product. That's why I always recommend Dove Men+Care products because they care about fatherhood and are pushing for paternity leave. Dove Men+Care celebrates a new definition of strength: one with care at its center. (Damn, that's good ad copy. Dove, you need some freelance work done?) Always market yourself.

Freelance gigs include photography, and there are some really talented dads who make this work as a source of income. From shooting weddings and family gatherings, a good photographer can make this something special. You have to put in the work to make it profitable, but I know a lot of dads who find work this way.

## 2. Obtaining a professional license.

This is one I want to touch on because with a little bit of work, getting the right license can start you a new side hustle. Notaries are freelance now, as are a lot of building inspectors. You can take a class, get a license, and then hang your digital shingle out on the web. By far, the biggest side hustle with a license is the real estate agent. I've known lots of dads who sell houses on nights and weekends. Mick had his license. He is also certified to judge barbecue contests. Mick is a smart son of a bitch.

## 3. IT work.

A bit obvious but expansive and flexible if this is your scene. From creating web pages to troubleshooting computers. This is also the side hustle that gets the most requests for free work, which is some bullshit. I mean, I get it a lot in writing, but with IT work the trolls come out of the woodwork. Larry is able to do IT work. Everyone is a best friend you never knew. Learn to say, "Fuck you, pay me." But if you need to advertise your services, I'm your man.

## 4. Professional freelance with specialized training.

These are your engineers, your marketing professionals, and me, your investigators. They require specialized experience, and usually more networking. The jobs come from large companies that don't want to pay benefits for one-off jobs, which is fine. Finding those jobs is also the most difficult, which is where the specific networking events come in.

It gives me a very specific skill set, particularly to lawyers in certain lawsuits. I did a stint as an expert witness. Take your past experience and open it up. From grant writing to coming up with a marketing campaign for a small business, use those skills as your side hustle.

> ## Because Dad Says So . . .
>
> *I embrace the fact that I'm home with my daughter. I have my separate workspace, but she has her own little desk in my office that she can sit at and color or play with Kinetic Sand if she wants to "go to work" with Dad. And if she comes in and interrupts a phone call, I let her say hello rather than pushing her out and closing the door. Most people on the other end of the line find it endearing more than anything else, and as she gets older, I want her to feel empowered to learn more about work life.*
>
> **Chris Kepner, father of one**

5. Education.

Tutoring and teaching English online are both real side hustles that pay a pretty good amount of money. They're flexible and there are companies that can hook you up directly with clientele, bringing down the amount of marketing you'll have to do. I've known several teachers who became at-home dads and were able to do this side hustle and make it work. There is a great demand for teaching English, which also means that there are a fair number of scam artists. Check everything out before you commit, but it is a great way to make money that offers flexibility.

### 6. Craftsmanship.

This one requires the most hustle as it's tough to get your name out there. These are your woodworkers, artists, and more creative types who make an actual product. This is Jake's side hustle. And a plug for him: His tables are fucking awesome. Seriously, he made one out of old bowling alley wood and it's marvelous.

He markets not only online but through word of mouth to designers, which I think is very clever. If you have a skill such as this, it's a viable side business that can make your next car payment. There are hard deadlines usually, but it's also flexible enough to work around your kids' schedules.

### 7. Accounting, bookkeeping, finance.

Highly specialized and in high demand. Small businesses may not have enough time to work payroll, taxes, and associated bookkeeping. If this is your niche, then it's easy enough to find a job. Yes, I know people who do this, including my own father at one time. Ha, how about that. This side hustle is generational. Both of my parents were accountants, which made them fabulously entertaining if you wanted to talk about numbers and get a good night's sleep.

I think I ended up with humor because no one in my house can tell a joke. My brother, Blake, whom I love dearly, sucks at telling jokes. Seriously, bro, it's not your thing. Maybe if you hadn't punched me that one time when I didn't change the channel, you would be funnier. That's probably it. Who's got the power now, big brother! I want to be Mario! Don't punch me for this.

There are side hustles out there for everyone, and finding them is easy thanks to the gig economy. They range from un-skilled manual labor to highly specialized degreed fields. There are entire books, websites, and podcasts that are designed to give you great information about how to start a side hustle and main-tain it. Just know that there is no such thing as easy money and they require actual, physical hustle. Nothing comes to you with-out working for it and taking the time to make it grow. Do your-self a favor and know your specific niche and really spend the time to figure out its ups and downs.

And remember, there are also a ton of shit heels and scam art-ists out there ready to eat your lunch. Some categories should just be avoided altogether—your mystery shoppers, envelope stuffers, and multilevel marketers.

## WHEN JOINING A MULTILEVEL MARKETING COMPANY GOES WRONG

I'm going to tell you a heartbreaking story about a dad who got in deep with an MLM company. I've warned you about how MLMs are scams, but an example may be the only way to drive the point home. This happened a long time ago.

He was a young guy, just starting a family. He had a wonder-ful wife who thought the world of him. The dad was good-looking, charismatic, and ambitious. He was one of those guys whom the whole world just roots for, but then he joined an MLM. When that happened, everything changed.

The dad fell for the same scams and false promises that I've told you about. Fancy toys, gigantic homes, and so much free-dom that it felt like the entire universe was there for the taking. But he never looked deeper than the flashy sales pitch.

Over time, the dad began to change, and he couldn't see it. The dream of what he could be started affecting his personality, which in turn began to affect his relationships. He became quick to anger at any failure or perceived slight, and selfishness crept into his personality. He spent more time trying to get his friends and family to join his MLM pyramid scheme. He believed in all the empty promises of the MLM.

Anyway, the dad hustled to get his friends to join. He knew that was the real way to gain power in an MLM, and that power was irresistible. The more people who joined, the more he gained. It was never about the product.

He missed dinners and neglected his wife. He would corner his friends and annoy the hell out of them with his overaggressive sales pitch. "Take advantage of this great opportunity! Control your own destiny!" Again and again and again. Soon, he was practically alone.

His marriage fell apart. His wife and kids left. The dad was devastated.

You would think that losing his family would have been a wake-up call. It wasn't. He went deeper down the MLM hole. And the further he went, the more important it was to recruit new members. He kept pushing, and his children suffered for it. They lost the father that they deserved.

Well, one day, after many years, the dad started to realize that maybe there was more to life. He tried to reconnect with his chil-dren, but they didn't even recognize who he had become. I don't think he recognized himself. His anger about his past and his ambition still caused him to go too far. Even with his kids, he couldn't give up the MLM habits.

He had two kids, a son and a daughter, who grew up pretty much without him. The more that the MLM demanded, the less time he had for his children. He was closer to a rumor of a dad than an actual positive force in their lives. He was with his son once, and things got heated.

"Join me or die!" he said to his son. Honestly, even I couldn't believe that one when I heard it.

He didn't do much better with his daughter, but he kept trying to reach out to her because that's what good dads do. We don't give up. He sent his daughter message after message. Sometimes those messages were discreet, like a feeling that travels through space and time. Other times they were more direct, like blowing up the planet Alderaan. None of it worked. It just pushed both his kids further away. Cutting off his son's right hand was a breaking point.

The dad knew it was a mistake but couldn't help himself. He knew that he wanted his children in his life. He knew that the value of family is worth more than the Empire. But after so many years, old habits die hard.

At the end, he finally realized how much his family meant to him and how much the Empire had taken. He made a decision that I wish he had made before the prequels. The dad threw his MLM sponsor, Palpatine, down a long shaft that had weirdo purple lightning for some reason. And there was his son, at the end, holding him at last.

This is what an MLM company can do to you and your family. It can leave you bald, staple-faced, and dying on an exploding Death Star.

And even though this happened a long, long time ago and in a galaxy far, far away, I think if we commit to this dad joke enough, we can all learn something. Here's to you, Anakin Sky-walker, father of two.

## GOING BACK TO WORK

There's going to come a time when all things end. The seasons, the years, and the laundry. I'm kidding, laundry is eternal. How-ever, eventually your time as an at-home dad may come to an end, and you're going to face a difficult question.

What now?

So let's hit on your fears first and get those out of the way. Yes, finding a job is going to take a while and at times be very frustrating. My best advice is to be easy on yourself. This is part of the deal with the stay-at-home dad gig. We talk about the sac-rifices many parents make to stay home with the kids. Well, this is it specifically staring you in the face in the form of an empty email inbox. Take it in stride and don't expect results quickly. Acknowledge that, accept it, and then move on to get shit done.

Second, if you are going back to the career you left, most likely you won't be making the same salary as you did before. In fact, this is one of the reasons many dads decide not to stay home with the kids. Their peers move up the career chain while we don't. And when we get back in, often it's at a lower position than what we are qualified for. It hurts, but it is the truth. I find that if we acknowledge the things we can't change at the very beginning, we can work to change the things we can.

But now is the fun part. You don't have to go back to doing

what you were doing before. If there was ever a time to take a chance or make a career change, this is it. I speak to this from personal experience. I took a chance on doing something I love. Do I make as much as I used to? Nope, not even close. And getting back to work definitely screwed with my head.

One day I was *the Ultimate Stay-at-Home Dad*! Then my youngest went to school, and I sat looking at the bus pull away. In that moment, all I had left were my memories. Time didn't stop, the kids grew up, and I was left alone. I could either wallow in that feeling or take a chance on something different. I decided to take the chance.

So those are your fears. The decision to go back to work is never easy, and you've got a lot of questions that I hope I'll be able to answer here. I won't tell you how to find a job, as there is no need to reinvent the wheel, but I will tailor those pieces of advice to our situation, the at-home dad.

But before we begin, let's give a shout-out to the moms on this one who have been asking these questions for generations. They are now reading this part, shaking their finger, and saying, "See, this is the shit we've had to figure out for years! Welcome to the club. Bring wine." Good on you, moms. We are going to borrow some of your answers.

Start by getting yourself ready to enter the job market. That means updating your social media profiles, checking to see if your skills are relevant, and then reworking your résumé to land your next job. Your whole purpose here is to sell yourself, which I know can be difficult for many people. Any kind of self-promotion, to me, feels almost slimy. You have to get over that shit. Think of yourself as the product, and a damn good one. Let's make it pretty for the buyer, the employers.

Consider taking classes at the local community college if that would help, as well as joining professional organizations and taking advantage of any learning opportunities that they have. Also, volunteering or working for a school system is a great way to add current experience to a résumé that has a blank spot. I've known plenty of dads who drive buses, run a lunchroom, or do IT work for a school.

And if you're looking for volunteer work, the National At-Home Dad Network is always looking for people to help. This is what I have done, and it sits nicely on my résumé.

### Because Dad Says So . . .

*You have to be willing to promote yourself. Really talk about your skills and frame everything as a positive. Know exactly what your employer is looking for and speak to that. Self-promotion isn't easy, but it gets better. So, reach out to headhunters or people you know. You never know when you'll turn a temporary job or a consulting gig into long-term employment.*

**Doug Zeigler, father of four**

Next, it's time to network, which feels about as slimy as self-promotion. But networking remains one of your greatest tools for finding your next job. Reach out to all your contacts to see what might be available or who can give you an introduction. Attend conferences if you can, especially if they are local, and print up business cards.

My wife is a great networker, so much so that she teaches a

class on it. We are going to borrow one of her pieces of advice. When attending an event, you can't leave until you have the names of three people and you've given your card out at least three times. That's your goal. I find I work better if I have a specific task.

Networking can also lead to freelance opportunities, consultant positions, or job leads. The more you network, the better your prospects will become. Again, I will use myself as the example. All my current paid writing gigs have come from networking. I knew a guy who knew another guy. To me, the networking is as important as the résumé.

Which brings us to the biggest two questions that all of us have asked:

1. How do I explain the gap on my résumé?
2. How do I answer the question during the interview?

## Because Dad Says So . . .

*When you address your time as an at-home dad in a cover letter, on a résumé, or in person, don't downplay it. You'll be doing yourself a huge disservice. Talk about it directly and with confidence. The skills that you have acquired as an at-home dad are valuable to a wide range of employers. Make them aware of how those can now be a benefit to them.*

**Tom Mahas, father of two**

All right, let's just say it and give something specific. The gap in your résumé should be explained in your cover letter. Don't try to hide it in the middle of a paragraph, but deal with it near the beginning. Here's your example so we can take the guesswork out of it.

> For the last several years, I had the amazing opportunity to be the primary caregiver to my family. It was a choice that has better prepared me to focus on the next step of my career. I've been able to improve my time-management skills, to multitask, and to handle high-pressure situations while remaining goal oriented.

There you go, the question is answered. Change it up to fit your situation more specifically, but at least you now have something to go on.

As for the actual interview, when they ask you about being an at-home dad, my best advice is to answer it clearly and quickly. Bring the answer back to the skills you've learned or improved upon, just like you did in the cover letter. Here's my go-to answer:

> My time as a stay-at-home dad was this really unique opportunity that I just couldn't pass up. It was a challenge but one that I found really allowed me to grow, and I'm really proud of the job I was able to do. Spending that time to create a stable home life now allows me to focus on the next stage of my career.

The next part of your answer should again bring all those skills you learned as an at-home dad and how they can now benefit the job you are applying for. Tailor the second part of that answer directly to your situation. Don't beat around the bush, and always sell yourself. You're a badass, and to make it through a stint in the trenches was hard work. Take credit for it and show the employer that not only are you proud of your contribution but it would benefit their company. So there you go. That's how you do it.

But . . .

If you want the joke answer, I'm going to do that, too, because I can't help myself.

You know what, Jim, thanks for asking that question about my time as a stay-at-home dad. You look handsome, by the way. Look, I can change a diaper one-handed in under twenty seconds. I've done that literally thousands of times. Big poops. Small squeakers. Curlicues. You name it, I've handled it. So, what I'm saying, Handsome Jim, is that I can get shit done.

Please, someone do that and let me know how it goes.

# CHAPTER 7

# MR. DINSMOOR AND THE BIG BALL OF TWINE

**WORDS OF WISDOM**

Just put the kids in the car and go.

*Charles Wasleski, father of two*

So, what do you guys do all day?" the random mom asked me. My dads group and I were at one of those play gyms that smell like disinfectant and socks. I got asked this question a lot, especially in the beginning. And as chill as I try to be, the question itself annoys me.

Moms seem fascinated by what dads do at home with the kids all day long. Almost as if there is no way I could know what I'm doing, nor have a nurturing instinct to do it well. It gets to be low-key insulting. I do all the same things that they do. I cook, clean, and drink wine at a bus stop while wondering if my man-boobs are getting too big.

I used to answer this question honestly, the same as moms, but I just have to protect my balls a little bit more. However, there came a time when I was just tired of answering. The question became irritating. So instead, I made shit up.

"Oh, we teach the children how to play catch with live hand grenades. Mess that up once and they learn the lesson," I said.

". . ."

The mom didn't even crack a smile. It bothers me when other people don't get my jokes. It's my one superpower.

"We see fun stuff, too. Graveyards, museums, the World's Largest Ball of Twine," I said, trying to add another joke. It just popped out of my head. Often, I think I should not talk at all and save myself a lot of awkward silences. Except this time, that didn't happen.

"Oh, you've been to Cawker City then?" she asked.

"Wait, what? What's in Cawker City?"

"The World's Largest Ball of Twine."

"That's a real thing?"

"Oh yeah, it's just right there off the highway. I thought that was what you were talking about."

I was just joking, and by pure coincidence, everything changed for me.

This was the summer before Vivi started kindergarten, and I was dreading it. By this time, she had been home with me for three years. Every burp, hiccup, and accidental cussword, I had been there for. And now, someone else was going to take her away from me. Inside, I started to feel nervous and a bit lost. I didn't think I would handle this well.

After that conversation with the random mom, who was just curious, I started to think. What had I done with those three years? What did I have to show for it? I had been all around town, but never farther than forty-five minutes away. And something as goofy as a large ball of twine, well, why hadn't I done that? This is when I discovered what the word *anything* really means. It means that I had the opportunity to go bigger, to have an adventure, to make those memories that will get me through the next hard day.

I became obsessed with seeing the World's Largest Ball of Twine. I did some research to see what else I could find. Turns out, there is a lot of weird shit in Kansas. Like, a lot. You have no idea. The World's Largest Decorative Plate, a rock that looks like a mushroom, the National Midget Auto Racing Hall of Fame—which is not what I thought it was. Turns out, they were referring to the small racing cars. Be that as it may, over the next six months I planned an overnight road trip to Cawker City, Kansas. Mick and the guys declined to go. No matter, I have a large dads group. I convinced Charles to go with me.

Charles and I loaded up his two kids, Kristina and David, into my minivan, and then the six of us took off on an adventure, one month before Vivi would be taken from me. The kids were close enough in age that it worked out well. Kristina is four years older than Vivi, but they got along really well. David is only a couple months older than Wyatt. But they were both potty trained, so that was a plus. In the morning, we set off.

Cawker City is three hours from where I live. But we had shit to see and memories to make! There was the Pony Express National Museum to explore. We saw a rock, and yup, it looked like a mushroom. I also got stuck in one of the midget racing cars, so thanks to the docent who helped me get out. Turns out, they are really small. And we also had to stop at the Garden of Eden.

The name, the Garden of Eden, makes you think of this idyllic garden with lush trees and forbidden fruit. That perhaps it's the last place that humanity actually lived the good life. I've heard that there are unlimited doughnuts in such a place. The Garden of Eden makes you think of calm and relaxation.

Get that shit right out of your head.

I am convinced, and remain so to this day, that the Garden of Eden in Lucas, Kansas, is where the zombie apocalypse is going to happen. Remember when I told you back in Chapter 5 to make sure you really do your research? This is why.

The Garden of Eden in Lucas is a Victorian home built by one Mr. S. P. Dinsmoor in 1904. Mr. Dinsmoor, a father, husband, and complete nutjob. I'm pretty sure he was a secret evil villain. He was also an artist.

His chosen medium was concrete, which I imagine was quite popular at the turn of the last century as far as artistic sculptures go. The house is a combination of limestone logs (is that a thing?) and concrete, which go together as naturally as peanut butter and straw. As in, you can eat it, but it doesn't look good.

Surrounding the house is his sculpture garden. Now, I'm no professional critic, but sometimes I think the term *art* is used a little loosely. A bored teenager gave our little troop a very detailed and informative tour. Fun fact: Did you know that nightmares can be made into abstract concrete construction and still scare the shit out of you? My son does now.

There is even a concrete zoo in the backyard, because every evil villain deserves a creepy-ass concrete zoo. I mean, it's part of the job perks, right?

Mr. Dinsmoor may have been off his rocker, but I've got to hand it to him. The home is over a hundred years old and still terrifying children to this day. That's quality craftsmanship.

> ## Because Charles Says So . . .
>
> *Those cages, man, I mean wow. They were so small and the first thought I had was I wonder who else he put in there. That guy wasn't right in the head.*

"And if you'll follow me," said Teenager McBoredface, "we will now visit the mausoleum of Mr. Dinsmoor."

So, serious question: What is the difference between a mausoleum and a crypt? It was at this point that I really wanted to know, and I started feeling bad for making Charles and his kids come to this with me. But good memories and bad memories are still memories, right?

The mausoleum was more like a stone shed that smelled like wet dog. We should have turned around, but honestly, I was having fun. All the kids appeared okay, and at the very least they'd have something to talk about with their therapist years down the road. It was small, too; we were all pretty much shoulder to shoulder. The only light was from the open door, and it was hard to see.

My plan was to see the gravestone or marker, whatever a mausoleum has, and then move on. I don't know, this was my first mausoleum, and I didn't know how graves were marked. Wyatt was in my arms, and Vivi was playing with Kristina behind me.

"And now we will see the body of Mr. Dinsmoor," our guide said.

It took a minute for that to register with me. Mr. Dinsmoor died all the way back in 1932. So that doesn't mean *body* body, yeah? The tour guide spoke as if he were announcing the specials at a diner. Yes, the clam chowder is excellent, and the seared salmon comes with a wonderful wine sauce. Also, we are going to see a dead body.

"Charles, maybe we should skip this part," I said to him.

But there's no time wasted with a bored tour guide. He's got shit to do and a script to follow. He turned on his flashlight.

"As you can see, Mr. Dinsmoor has been perfectly preserved in the property he built."

First off, I'm calling bullshit. Second, I would appreciate a little more of a heads-up.

Behind a sheet of plexiglass in a concrete "coffin," there was the dead body of Mr. S. P. Dinsmoor, dead for nearly eighty years. Artist. Father. Evil villain. And for the record, the caulking game at the Garden of Eden could use a little bit of work. For some reason, the dad in me noticed the nice quarter-inch gap between the plexiglass and the coffin before I noticed Zombie Dinsmoor grinning at me and my children.

Mr. Zombie Dinsmoor seems to now have a very serious skin condition, but at least he's happy. Wispy white hair goes down to his shoulders, and his eyes are closed, at least for now. His suit looked good, though.

To the kids' credit, they didn't freak out. I mean, as far as I know. Vivi said, "Gross," and then went back outside to play tag with Kristina among the empty zoo cages, which I'm now not so sure were for animals. Wyatt and David leaned over to look as Charles and I sat there not really knowing what to do.

"Thank you for coming," said the tour guide. "Please stop by the gift shop on the way out." We did not stop by the gift shop.

We left just in case Zombie Dinsmoor decided now was the time to wake up and bring about the End Times.

Eventually, in early evening, we made it to our campsite near Cawker City, Kansas. We set up our tents and headed into town to have dinner and see the twine, the whole reason for this trip.

Cawker City is a small midwestern town with a population a bit over four hundred. It's the kind of place where directions are given in the terms of "over yonder" and "one over." Sixty-year-old facades line the main street in a picture postcard of what Middle America looks like. It was late evening, and the shadows of the buildings disappeared into the prairie grass that surrounds the town. It also has only one restaurant.

### Because Charles Says So . . .

*When we first saw Cawker City, it was late in the afternoon and the main street was deserted. It was like an eerie movie set. I half expected to see some guy come running down the street screaming about a mysterious chemical spill at the secret laboratory and that "they" had gotten out. Run for your lives!*

And I use the term *restaurant* as loosely as Zombie Dinsmoor used the term *art*. The building in front of Charles and me could be called a restaurant in the same way that a donkey could be called a horse. From a distance, a donkey and a horse look similar. But up close, what you notice is that the donkey is a smaller, meaner version of the noble steed. I'm just saying the restaurant had a donkey aura about it. There was an OPEN sign on the front that seemed more of a suggestion than an invitation.

The building looked like someone had taken a couple of double-wide mobile homes and cut off one wall on the long side and stuck them back together. The patio was surrounded by a tin fence that reminded me of a barn roof. There probably was a lot of duct tape construction going on to get this place up to code.

"Ya know," I said to Charles as we sat in the minivan. "If there is a bar fight in there, I don't think I can hang. If things go south, take the kids and run." This is what I do when I'm nervous and tired. I make jokes to cut the tension.

"Kids gotta eat," Charles said. "We didn't bring any food for camp, and the next place is forty miles away. It's either here or we are eating floor-crushed potato chips and crotch graham crackers."

In the back, the kids had started getting wild. That point that every parent knows, where they go from hungry to hangry. On the short trip from our campsite just down yonder and one over from the highway, Vivi had started throwing Goldfish crackers at the back of my head.

"Let's head in," Charles said. This is why I like adventuring with him. He's flexible when things go bad or when the un- planned happens. Sometimes he's quiet and awkward, which com- plements my extroverted nature. We make a good team. However, he's a bit on the smaller side, and I'm not sure how good he would be in a bar fight. With that said, though, he ran his kids' school PTA for years, so I'm sure he knows how to fight dirty.

The door to the restaurant opened up on rusty hinges and we walked through. The inside made the outside look like a well- thought-out plan of construction. Card tables sat around the small space randomly and were bordered by metal chairs that would seem more at home at a backyard barbecue. The smell of grease was so heavy in the air that I was pretty sure I could now part my nose hair or give it a nice spike. And there was a bar where eight burly men turned and stared at Charles, me, and our kids.

For a guy who lives in a world of awkward moments, who truly embraces them, this was too much even for me. Normally, I can fit in just about anywhere. I'm a charismatic bastard. I'm loud and dramatic with a flair for presentation. But here, nope, totally out of my element. None of the men said anything. Not a word.

Most were older and had long beards. They wore overalls that were covered in the earth that they worked. Sweat-stained hats shielded eyes that never looked away. Vivi grabbed my leg, and I imagine Kristina was doing the same to Charles. It really was one of those moments that seem frozen in time. We stood there. They stared.

After what seemed like days, a smaller man came from behind the pack at the bar. He was shorter than me and younger than the other men. His arms looked ropy, like the kind that are used to throwing hay bales around. He didn't have a beard but hadn't shaved in a while either. A few long hairs waved off his chin. As he got close, I could see his magnified eyes through his thick glasses. He stopped a foot in front of me, didn't say a word, and just looked.

Rarely do I find myself speechless. I can talk to anyone, anywhere, about anything for hours. It's part of my nature. But here? I got nothing. The man took a step closer and invaded my personal space. I have no idea how this got weirder, but it did. His smell reminded me of a fire pit next to a diesel engine. It was as heavy as the grease. So I did the first thing that came to mind, which sometimes doesn't work out so well.

"Hi!" I said like an overenthusiastic idiot. I was joking earlier about a bar fight, but as this man stood in front of me I couldn't help but have visions of that movie *Road House* with Patrick Swayze where everyone just starts throwing punches for no reason in a crowded bar out in the sticks. That is what I felt like. It seems silly now, of course, but then? I just wasn't sure what was going to happen next.

That's when the man hugged me.

## Because Charles Said So . . .

*When Shannon got hugged, I thought,* How quick can I make it to the car? *Not to ditch him, but you know, this was weird. I was going to take his kids with me, though. For the most part when it happened, I was speechless and stunned.*

Of all the possibilities that were going through my head, this was not one of them. My mind went from *Road House* to *Deliverance* in about two seconds. And I don't mean some sort of quick man hug with a nice slap on the back. I mean a full-on hug. The kind you would give your mom after you haven't seen her in a while and have had some troubles in your life. The kind of hug where a head rests on your chest and you want to pat the person's hair and let them know that everything is going to be okay. I stood there for a second, with Wyatt in my arms squished between us, as the man rubbed my back a little bit. I had no idea what was going on or what to do. So, he just . . . hugged. For a really long time. And then I made a decision.

Fuck it, I hugged him back. Damn right. When a grown man hugs you like that, maybe he really needs it. Who am I to deny that? I'm a nurturing motherfucker, and more than anyone, I know the power of a good hug. So, I said screw it and gave back as good as I got. I put my son down and then went in for round two. I'm a big believer that hugs make the world a better place.

A few of the bar guys got off their stools and headed our way.

"Howdy!" said one of the men.

It turns out that the people of Cawker City, Kansas, are the most wholesome sons of bitches on the face of this planet, and I count that experience as one of the best I've ever had in my life.

Charles and I were ushered to one of the card tables and given no menu by our new friends. This was a no-menu kind of place. Our host gave us a rundown of what could be cooked up, which was no more than burgers and hot dogs. And beer, of course. Fantastic beer. One of the best beers I've ever had.

I'm not sure how, and I'm not sure why, but I felt at home and welcomed. For a stay-at-home dad, this is a pretty big deal. That feeling doesn't come easy out in the world, but they have it in abundance in Cawker City. Our drinks were served in dirty Solo cups, but I had my adventure bag with me, so no big deal. Several of the bar dudes pulled up their stools to our table and started asking questions.

"Where y'all from?" said one.

"Camping over at the state park?" asked another.

They wanted to know everything about us, and when they found out we were stay-at-home dads, they loved it even more. It brought back memories they had of their own kids.

"When my boy was young" came up a lot, and it was usually followed by "Before my kids got married."

We did this for the rest of the evening. We all talked about our kids, about our lives, and about being fathers. It remains one of those surreal moments that have defined how I look at the rest of my life. Here are these guys who welcome strangers for no reason other than kindness. Their eyes sparkle when they tell the stories of their own kids, and you can tell that they miss the children who are now grown.

Charles and I ate greasy burgers, drank a few fantastic beers, and listened to all the advice they wanted to give about their time in the trenches. We also got the history of the World's Largest Ball of Twine. It weighs in at over nineteen thousand pounds, and every year the town has a festival where even more twine is added. Also, a tip, don't call the ball of twine a ball of string. They don't take that too kindly.

## Because Charles Says So . . .

*It's a big ball of twine. That's what it is. What do you want me to say? It's twine.*

After dinner, a few walked us down to the ball of twine. It stands over ten feet tall and is so heavy now that the bottom bows out so it looks like a ball is being cupped by a twine bowl. Charles and I took pictures, which still hang on my adventure wall. The kids ran around, and I just watched. I remember smiling a lot. I knew this was the memory I had been hunting for. This is when I figured out what *anything* really meant.

We went back to camp and the next morning headed home. We almost ran out of gas near the Land of Oz Museum but luckily found something with twelve miles left in the tank.

Ten years later, as I was beginning to write this book, I did this trip again. Mick and Larry went with me as they had not come the first time. I wanted to make those same memories with my youngest son, Ollie. What I know now, and not then, is that the experiences were as much for me as they were for the kids.

I also wanted to go back to that restaurant, and I needed to talk to the hugger. I wanted to let him know he would be in a book. On the way we again stopped at the Garden of Eden to pay our respects to Mr. Zombie Dinsmoor. He's still very dead, and the plexiglass has been properly sealed. I'll let you know when he wakes up, though. Just look for a fiery vortex to hell.

The restaurant has changed a lot since the last time I was there. It looks normal, or maybe it always did and in my memory I've built it up to be something nefarious. Inside, card tables have been replaced for a more family-friendly dining experience. In fact, the whole joint now seems like the place to be for families in Cawker City on a Saturday night. The place was packed. Farmers at the bar have been replaced by people waiting for a table.

I walked up to the bar and spoke to the bartender, eager to find my hugger. I described him the best I could. The bartender asked why.

"Well, actually, he's going to be in a book, and I wanted to let him know."

A middle-aged man nearby overheard my question and stood up.

"What kind of book is it?"

"A book about dads," I said.

"Well, the guy you're looking for has moved out of town."

I figured that was the case, but it was worth a shot.

"What do you have to do to get in your book?" the man asked.

"Well, he gave me a hug," I said, and laughed as the kids walked around. Vivi and Wyatt had no memory of this place. Mick and

Larry had heard me tell this story a hundred times, and I was wondering in that moment if they could reconcile what I'd told them to what they saw now.

"So, to get in your book, I just have to give you a hug?" asked the man.

"Apparently," I said.

The man, who as it turned out used to be the mayor of Cawker City, got up from his chair where he was eating dinner with his family and gave me a huge bear hug. And just as before, it was awesome. So, there you go, Mr. Mayor, you're in a book. Thank you for the hug.

This trip, the first one, was special for me. It was the beginning of what we now call the dads trip. Just kids and dads, no moms. Not that the moms wouldn't be welcome, but I think they appreciate the time alone. I'm not sure what they do when Mick, Larry, Jake, Mike, and I are gone. Maybe they eat cheese and have pillow fights. But these trips have turned into more than just trips for us.

They are the highlight of the kids' summer. We've been doing them for ten years now and I look forward to them every year. It's those memories. It always comes down to them. At the time of this writing, some of our oldest kids are about to start high school. Ollie went on his first dads trip when he was four months old.

The trips have gotten bigger as well. What started as a quick one night with Charles and me has turned into a whole-week adventure with all the dads. Our biggest group was around thirty people. It takes me six months or more to plan them, and I usually start right after Christmas.

I have played baseball with a couple of nuns on the Field of Dreams in Iowa. I have hand-fed buffalo from the back of a wagon and seen the World's Largest Pair of Overalls in Nebraska. I have been to the birthplaces of Johnny Cash, John Wayne, and Captain Kirk. I have seen a second ball of twine in Minnesota. In Oklahoma, the kids learned how to throw an ax. So if you are in Middle America and see a caravan of minivans, it might be Mick, Larry, Jake, Mike, and me.

I use every trick I know to get ready. I pinch pennies, plan, and make it through that daily grind. Every day, I cook and clean and run kids to sports. Sometimes I coach. I do my side hustle in between my parenting to make a little extra money to afford the trip in the first place. It's interesting to me to see how it has evolved over the years.

The kids are no longer small, and they don't think of themselves as playgroup friends. They grew up together and continue to do so. They consider each other siblings, regardless of which family they are with. They hop from car to car on the road. Mike's car is officially the "fun" car for some reason, and they all seem to fight for space in there with him.

At stops, they peel off into their own groups. They have their own inside jokes, and stories that I have no idea about. They are building memories where I'm in the background. I didn't expect my dads group to be like this, but I know that I'm lucky it is. And I know my kids are better for it, but I don't think they truly understand what the dads trip means. To them, it's something fun to do in the summer with their friends. They think we all get together on the road because that's what they've always done. They think this trip is for them.

Mike, Larry, Jake, Mike, and I know better, though.

The trip is for us.

> ## ☰ *Because Charles Says So . . .*
>
> *Get out of your house and have an adventure. Find your*
> *friends and your support system. It really helps. With all*
> *the trips we took, that was a time to bond. Not just with*
> *our kids, but with other dads, too. Man, we did so much. I*
> *remember pitching baseball practice on the Field of*
> *Dreams to all the kids on one of those trips. So yeah, just*
> *put the kids in the car and go.*

## LAST CALL

Much of the advice given to dads is, honestly, hot garbage. It is
often condescending and written as if we are complete morons.
Moreover, it makes the assumption that we don't want to be
around our children in the first place, and that by doing so, we
are doing Mom a favor. The advice given to stay-at-home dads is
even worse. In researching this book, I took a look around to see
what specifically had been said and if it had changed since the
last time I looked years ago.

One popular article featured a dad who couldn't get his children to school on time. These weren't babies, mind you, but
double-digit-aged kids who could get dressed and make their
own breakfast. And even if I give it the benefit of the doubt as an
attempt at humor, it perpetuates the idea that all dads are so in-
competent that even the most basic tasks are beyond us. To me,
this is punching down and a cliché that needs to go away.

Another article, written more specifically for the stay-at-home dad, suggested finding a group that you could belong to. I was hopeful, but as I read I became angry again. The advice was to join a moms group and sit silently out of the way until you are accepted. I'm not joking here, that was the real advice.

And rarely do you see anything talking about our mental health other than a side note. One such author suggested that we "toughen up."

That is why I wrote this book. This is what I needed when I first started. Not only as a stay-at-home dad, but just as a dad. The idea that I wouldn't want to be involved in every part of my child's life never felt right to me, and to pretend otherwise in some sort of show of masculinity angered me. To be blunt, it's bullshit.

I think that my wife is pretty tired of my railing against some of the things that I read. At night as we talked about this book and my research, I would get so worked up that I couldn't sleep. I was "authentically mad," as she said. The phrase has stuck with me throughout this whole process.

I wanted a book that I would read, that had actionable advice that I could use as well as some jokes that could speak to my experience. I wanted something that didn't talk down to me. I wanted a book that would take my natural skills as a dad and utilize them in a day-to-day way. I didn't want to go to a mall playground or complete flowery crafts that I could post on Pinterest. I wanted to build a trebuchet. I wanted a book that I could see myself in and not be told to sit in a corner and be quiet until I'm accepted. Fuck that.

There are a few things that I want you to keep in mind going forward. First, I recognize how lucky I am. Not only can I afford to stay home with the kids, but I happened upon a group of guys who were in the same place in life as I was. Fathers who made no apologies for what they did. They had kids the same age as mine and wanted a place where we could ask the questions we couldn't ask anywhere else. Ironically, it was isolation that brought us together. And for whatever reason, we all connected on . personal level that grew into something more. The fact that our wives also connected is probably more unusual than the five of us getting together in the first place. Finding ten adults who all enjoy each other's company is pretty rare.

Second, it is not my intention here to bag on moms. I take a few shots, sure, but moms in general have a real shitty deal in my opinion. No matter what decision they make, they are judged for it. Work, stay home, whatever. And it is obvious to me that most do the heavy lifting when it comes to childcare, which is also bullshit. For moms in general, to me at least, there never seems to be a right answer. A lot of what I've learned, I've learned by watching them. And there are those moms who took me under their wing to show me the ropes.

When my father was passing, I had to take a late flight back to my hometown. The kids were with me because I wanted to give them a chance to say goodbye. My wife would follow us the next day and honestly, we didn't have the money for her to fly down with us. In the airport, there was a mom traveling with a two-year-old herself to the same city. For a reason I will never understand, she saw that I needed help.

For that flight, as Vivi and Wyatt sat in other seats, that mom paired Ollie with her own kid. I provided the videos and she brought the snacks. Our two boys shared a seat on a late-night flight. The mom and I had never met, and it was completely random, but she showed me kindness when I needed it. I want you to know that there are more moms out there like that than there are the screamers. The screamers are just more fun to watch. The world loves drama.

Finally, you need to understand that my successes are built on a mountain of failures. In fact, this whole book is almost a high-light reel of my worst moments. I've burnt more dinners than I care to remember. And many of my screwups have happened in very public ways. There is nothing like your brand-new daughter throwing up all over a comforter set at a department store in front of a crowd. This whole book has been humbling for me to write, and there were many parts I didn't want to share.

But I did write them, because I needed you to see me as I truly am, not as some superhero who is perfect and has all the answers. I'm hoping that you can learn from my mistakes, but as you do, realize there is no such thing as a perfect parent, and you should not try to live up to that ideal. To do so, and to believe that everything in this book happened quickly, would be over-whelming. This is the collective experience of guys who have been doing this for decades. Please, don't compare yourself to any of us, or to anyone, for that matter.

I've made it a point to get advice from a diverse set of dads here alongside my own advice. Take what you need and ditch the rest. Or even better, take a pencil and add your own advice for future generations. My way certainly isn't the only way, and sometimes I'm wrong as hell. Actually, I'm wrong a lot.

Not every day is going to be an adventure. Many days are going to be a downright disaster. That's cool; that's the way it goes. If you do this long enough, you'll have your own memories to write about.

Mick likes to say that he always does what works for his

family, and I think that is great advice to live by. I have days when I can barely function, but I am doing what I believe is best for those who I love. That love includes Mick, Larry, Jake, and Mike. Now they are going to be all weird about this when they read that here, but so be it. Screw those guys, accept my affection!

Do the best you can and realize that it is good enough. Cook the meals and clean the house, stretch the budget, and get your people around you. Join a dads group and take care of your mental health. It needs more attention than you think. Take the bad days one at a time and remember the good ones. And most of all, enjoy the adventure. You've got this.

After all, here at the end, you are the Ultimate Stay-at-Home Dad.

# ACKNOWLEDGMENTS

There are times when you are writing that you believe you are alone. It's not until the end that you realize that was never the case. One of the best parts of writing a book is thanking the people who helped make it happen. Let's do this!

I once described my agent, Chris Kepner, as the literary version of Conan the Barbarian, on the hunt for a kingdom for this book. I stand by that. I am forever grateful for his friendship, knowledge, and tireless work to make this book a reality. One day, I'm going to have to get him a sword. I know a dad who could make that happen.

Thanks to both Jen Mann and James Breakwell, who gave me early encouragement that not only could I write, but I should.

A big thanks to James Jayo, who first put the question to me: "What if you added advice to your book?" I said I would if I could still swear. He took that, swear words and all, and championed this book into existence. I owe him a beer and barbecue one day.

Elda Rotor, my editor, was the best guide I could have possibly hoped for. She may not know this, but she encouraged me to write the parts that were the most difficult. To be open and honest when hiding behind a joke was much more comfortable. She pushed me in the best way possible and the book you hold in your hands wouldn't have happened without her confidence in me. "You will help people, Shannon," she once said. It was that simple statement that gave me courage when I didn't feel any. Thank you, Elda. You will always have a spot on my adventure wall.

To my Penguin team, I owe both my sincere thanks and my humble apologies. Semicolons and em dashes are my mortal enemies. It takes a special person to copy edit a dick joke, and I hope I didn't make you reconsider your careers. Megan Gerrity, Scott Alexander Jones, and Angelina Krahn—thank you for making me sound way better than I am. Elizabeth Vogt did a great job of keeping me on task and will one day explain to me what yacht rock is all about. Sabrina Bowers blew me away with the interior design, and Gregg Kulick produced a cover so spot-on that I was speechless when I saw it for the first time. So, to everyone at Penguin, thank you for giving this dad book a chance to visit the world.

Thank you to my humor people: The Dead Pigeons, Andrew Knott and Jared Bilski, who spent hours talking about the jokes with me. And thank you to Lucie Frost, Jen Freymond, Kristen Mulrooney, Rebekah Iliff, and Catherine Weingarten, who tore every joke apart in a good way.

We're on a roll, let's keep going with the best smug buttholes I have the honor to call my friends: Mike Blackwelder, Britany Wilmes, and James Burford. They are literary as fuck and read every page before anyone else. With the gentleness of a sledgehammer, they let me know when I was holding back. Thank you so very, very much.

I could write another book thanking all the other dads who made this book possible. I interviewed over sixty of them to make sure I was giving the best advice I could. They allowed me to pick their brains and ask endless questions. But more than that, they shared their own experiences without reservation. A special thanks to all of them and to Dad 2.0, the National At-Home Dad Network, and City Dads Group, as they were the driving force behind this book. Thanks, Dads.

Speaking of dads, thanks to Mick, Larry, Jake, and Mike. I find myself, for the first time ever, at a loss for words. Your friendship has been life changing, and I honestly don't know how to tell you how much you mean to me. Is this weird now? I don't care. I love you guys and thank you.

And, of course, to my wonderful wife, Erin. She once asked me, "When are you going to stop fucking around and write?" That was the moment that everything really happened. She not only spent countless hours at night listening to me talk about character development and chapter construction, but also knew when to lay a hand on my forearm to help me find my center. She has been, and always will be, my true north. She is my lobster.

Vivi, Wyatt, and Oliver—you make me a better man every day. Without question, there is no one that I owe more to than you three. I will spend the rest of my life trying to give you as much as you have already given me. But also, please stop breaking shit. That would be cool.

And because I'm taking this opportunity to make a fucking point: To Ava, Julian, Sidda, Bodhi, Isa, Emma, Jack, and Bo—Uncle Shannon has put your name in a book. Beat that Uncle Jordan! Who's the best uncle now, Mr. I-Invented-Bacon? Who the hell tells kids that, anyway? My kids still think you did. Eat a dick.

Also, thank you to Uncle Jordan because Erin says I can't end this by insulting her brother. I am the best uncle, though.